W9-CJR-734

# FORTY-FIVE MINUTES
# PAST EIGHT

WARD MOREHOUSE

# Forty-five Minutes Past Eight

THE DIAL PRESS

NEW YORK · MCMXXXIX

PRINTED IN THE UNITED STATES OF AMERICA
BY THE HADDON CRAFTSMEN, INC.

To  F.C.S.

# CONTENTS

# FORTY-FIVE MINUTES
# PAST EIGHT

## Peachtree to Broadway

THE TRAIN FOR THE NORTH LEFT ATLANTA'S PEACHTREE
station at 2:30 P.M., late fall of 1919, and I had lower 6.
The next noon, bewilderedly, I got my first glimpse of
New York, registered at the Hotel McAlpin, hurried to
the *Tribune* office in Nassau Street, was instantly hired at
$50 a week, and within an hour was off on my first assign-
ment. I was to interview Marcus Garvey about his dream
ship to Africa. There'd been high talk of the founding of
a black republic; Garvey was being hailed as a New Moses
and a Black Christ. I eventually got to Harlem but not to
Marcus Garvey. My reception wasn't cordial and persist-
ence resulted in my being almost catapulted down the
stairway. New York's transportation complexities seemed
too overpowering at that moment and I took a cab to the
Penn station. There wasn't a train for forty minutes.
Somewhat desperately, I returned to Nassau Street and told
City Editor Macfarland that I didn't like it and was going
back South. Macfarland grinned. He explained that they
generally tried Harlem on reporters from the "Sa-outh,"
as he called it, and perhaps I might fare better in China-

3

town. The next morning's *Tribune*, not then wedded to the *Herald*, carried my account of a dinner in a little up-one-flight-and-turn-to-the-right restaurant in Doyers Street. There it was, exactly as the copy was written. Test enough, I thought. I wired the *Atlanta Journal* that I would not be back.

I didn't see Broadway by night until the evening of the second day. A fattish man named Perrin, who was on his way up, was the Night City Editor. He had a Scotch-Irish assistant, B. O. McAnney, and they presented a far stronger combination than the day side team of Macfarland & McKenna. I was given a "good-night" around 8:30, took the East Side express at Brooklyn Bridge, obediently followed the Green Line through the Grand Central's underground web, and shuttled westward to Times Square. So, on that near-zero night, I reached the curb which had been promised me by an itinerant Shakespearean reader several years before. But he, beset by urgent financial difficulty, got mixed in his geography and left me sitting forlornly upon a park bench in Roanoke.

Broadway blazed and sputtered. Forty-second Street was crammed with playhouses. The White Way signs, not nearly so given to the petulant gymnastics of nowadays, were on full. The marquees of the theaters spelled out their magic wares: Fay Bainter in "East is West." Frank

Bacon in "Lightnin'." Ina Claire in "The Gold Diggers."
The Barrymores in "The Jest." Lillian Lorraine in "The
Blue Devil." . . . I walked, jaywalked, gazed, gaped. The
setting was new, but all the names were familiar. I'd never
been north before but the theater had come south and I
knew it by heart. I'd seen all the touring troupes since the
age of twelve. Road shows, resident stock companies and
vaudeville acts liked the Southern jaunts. My town was
Savannah, prior to Atlanta, and the troupers from New
York played the red-brick and terra cotta structure on
Chippewa Square, Bull Street. David Warfield, John Drew,
William Hodge, Maude Adams, Billie Burke and Lew
Dockstader. The Baldwin-Melville Stock. The Schiller
Players. Alexander Leftwich's Players. Henrietta Brown
and Company. Adelaide Thurston came along regularly.
So did Norman Hackett and Tim Murphy and Emma
Bunting and Paul Gilmore. I saw "Mrs. Wiggs of the Cab-
bage Patch" in a skating rink and "The Clansman" under
canvas. I read, unfailingly, the Sunday *Times*, the *Green
Book* (Channing Pollock), the *Theatre Magazine*, *Variety*,
*The Clipper*, *Munsey's*, the *Smart Set*, the *Dramatic Mirror*, *Harper's*, *Scribner's*, *Life* (James A. Metcalfe). I de-
voured every printed play obtainable, and got through
two, three, maybe four, histories of the American theater.

I knew the drama's lore from the Hallams and Dunlap
to Augustin Daly, A. M. Palmer and the Frohmans. I

knew about the Wallacks, about Forest & Macready, Laura Keene's Varieties, Niblo's Gardens and Harrigan & Hart; about Oscar (the Great) Hammerstein, Koster & Bail's, Hurtig & Seamon, Brady & Grismer, Wagenhals & Kemper, Sothern & Marlowe, Stair & Havlin, Nixon & Zimmerman, Corse Payton, Armstrong & Mizner and Bim the Button Man; James A. Herne, James O'Neill, Joseph Jefferson, Ada Rehan, Denman Thompson, William Gillette, Richard Mansfield, Belasco, Bernhardt, the Drews and the Barrymores, William Winter, and K. and E. and their all-powerful syndicate, which came to be challenged by the upstart brothers Shubert from upstate New York.

Olga Nethersole played "Sappho," shocked press and public, was dragged into court and Sapphos instantly flooded the land. Mrs. Leslie Carter swung from a bell in "The Heart of Maryland," moved on to a triumph in "Zaza" and David Belasco, with tears in his larynx, told a first-night audience that she was the happiest woman in the world. Ethel Barrymore fluttered into stardom via Fitch's "Captain Jinks of the Horse Marines." Maude Adams captivated theaterdom with her Lady Babbie. Sam S. Shubert, brightest of the three brothers, lost his life in a railway wreck. Clara Bloodgood, at the height of her fame, blew out her brains in a Baltimore hotel. And Mrs. Fiske found a play, one written by a brilliant young man just out of Harvard by the name of Edward Sheldon. All of this, all the details of it, I knew, just as I knew the later-day lore. Now, as I stood at the Broadway and Forty-second Street curb, I had the feeling that I was among friends—old friends. . . . Edith Day in "Irene," Olive Tell, beauty of the day, in "Civilian Clothes." Helen MacKellar, in "The Storm." To the south, the red-and-gold Empire sheltered Miss Barrymore in "Déclassé." To the north, the Palace, vaudeville's pinnacle, just where I'd expected it to be, and giving its ratings in nightly incandescence to William Rock, to Blossom Seeley, to Joe E. Howard; also to Leon Errol, Belle Baker, Irene Franklin, Grace Larue and the ever-recurrent Rooney & Bent.

It seemed an area with which I had long been familiar—theater-fronts, street intersections, electric displays. There was the Astor, whose bulk is so impressive to one beholding Broadway for the first time; the gaudy Knickerbocker —no chairs in the lobby, King Cole in the bar and Caruso in the house, occupying sixteen rooms. It all fitted snugly into my own mental pattern long before devised. But somehow, as I wandered northward, jostling and being jostled, I half expected to come upon a statue of Charles Frohman in the heart of Longacre Square or a bust of Belasco, of the turn-around collar and the thick, silken white locks, on a pedestal at the entrance of Childs. I kept walking, kept gaping and, finally, unable to resist longer, paid for standing room at the Gaiety, my first time inside a New York theater. I was there just in time to hear Lightnin' Bill Jones tell the one about how he drove a swarm of bees across the desert in the dead of winter and didn't lose a bee.

But back to Atlanta and the post-war delirium. . . . I'd gone to the *Journal*, its leading paper, after a few months of $9-weekly reporting on the *Savannah Press*. The Atlanta of 1918-20 was a good theater town; it had always been a good news town, right on through the Sherman's time to the Leo Frank case and the furor over the Ku Klux. During the year of 1919 Atlanta, serving as a port of entry for all the south, swarmed with homecoming uniformed men. Fringed by military settlements— Camp Gordon and Fort McPherson—it was as hero-minded as a city could be and the commotion endured long after the armistice. Soldiers, soldiers, soldiers roamed Peachtree Street. Some were staying, some were passing through and just looking. Many had decorations, many were on crutches. Atlanta, like all America, was hero receiving. The flow of the olive drab was so continuous it seemed that a great gangplank had been stretched from the Hoboken pier to Five Points. Parades. Receptions. Teas. Dinners. Speeches. Laughter. Tears. Songs. Kisses. It was a delirium for those who had come back and for those who never would; for the whole and the hearty, the lame and the maimed, the heroic and unheroic. Bugles and bands. Re-employment and readjustment. The Y.M.C.A., and the K. of C. and the Red Cross. Citizens' committees, post-war drives, subscriptions, contributions, speeches. Formalities were disregarded and forgotten. The city's exclusive homes flung open their doors. Service men scraped their boots upon the thresholds of the Capital City Club and the Piedmont Driving Club; they danced with debs and sub-debs in the tiled and palmed lounge of the Georgian-Terrace. Atlanta's welcome-homing bore all the fervency that had gone into its good-bying. A man in uniform, until the frenzy was past, was a man in hero's garb. Georgia's capital, which had undergone cataclysms, was at its best in fever-pitch moods, in moments of unrepressions, whether its emotions were loosened by Bobby Jones, Alexa Sterling or the returning horde of the A.E.F.

The youthful Bobby Jones, now internationally known, went on with his dazzling golf at East Lake. The Metropolitan Opera came and went. The Atlanta Theater booked in the road shows and the Forsythe played big-time vaudeville—or nearly so. Atlanta continued its chanting of war-time melodies. Young Georgians who had gone abroad as corporals and sergeants were now being addressed as lieutenants and captains, and bearing up under it. The adventure over, their patriotism tested, their duty done, the town's clubmen, including some of the wealthy and perennially eligible bachelors, lolled on the terrace of the Capital City Club; Mrs. Coolidge rocked on the veranda of the Georgian-Terrace and the bands played "Mademoiselle

from Armentières" and "Over There" and "Long, Long
Trail A-Windin'" and "Where Do We Go From Here,
Boys?" and always, as a climax number, broke into the
strains of "Dixie."

In the meantime, I'd married. My wife was nineteen,
and just graduated from Agnes Scott College at Decatur,
six miles out of Atlanta. She, too, was Georgia-born—
dark, pretty and the most completely unselfish person I
have ever known. We'd known each other a long time,
had gone to high school together and had lived a block
apart in Savannah. She was a niece of the Georgia jurist,
Judge Roan, who presided over the long and bitter and
harrowing trial of Leo Frank. Judge Roan, in reflections
of later years, told her that he had never been convinced
of the guilt of Frank, against whom a Georgia jury returned a verdict of guilty of murder in the first degree.

I was now wondering about New York and how to find
a place there, just as I had begun planning an invasion of
the larger field, Atlanta, soon after W. G. Sutlive gave me
my start on the *Savannah Press*. The *Atlanta Journal's*
men had been notably successful in the north. Grantland
Rice, Innis Brown, Don Marquis, Jacques Futrelle. There
were legends of them, and of many others, who had done
newspaper work in the vicinity of Five Points, the Georgia
capital's equivalent of Broadway and Forty-second Street.
Certainly, legends of Keats Speed, an able and resourceful
managing editor, who had retained his standing as a gentle-

man despite the obvious handicap of having been sent into town by Hearst; of Jake Gortatowsky, Bill Farnsworth, McCaw of the *Georgian*, Tracy Mathewson, demon photographer; Bill Seabrook, Mike Clofine, Britt Craig, dashing news-getter, and of a somewhat mysterious young newsman named Harold Ross, who established himself as a crack police reporter and then suddenly vanished, saying good-bye to nobody. When Atlanta next heard of him he was in France and he wasn't a reporter any longer. He was an editor. His paper was the *Stars and Stripes*.

Several of us on the *Journal* staff had New York yearnings; we were also possessed by fiction-writing. I'd written some two dozen plays which had reached production via amateur and semi-professional players of Georgia, but the short-story field, save for contributions to school publications, was a new medium. In the spring of 1919 my bride and I lived at Atlanta's best hotel—the Georgian-Terrace. A large inside room, no bath, which the late Jesse Couch gave us at $10 a week and suggested that we not mention the rate. The Metropolitan Opera stars descended upon Atlanta in April, flocked to the Terrace, and the city went once more into one of its artistic orgies. I didn't go to the opera, but dressed around 11 P.M. and mingled with the Terrace mob. From 8 until 11 o'clock on every evening of that week I bent over a typewriter in my seventh-floor room. With all the city at the Auditorium, enraptured by "Lucia" or "La Bohème" or "Traviata," I pounded out my first short story designed for professional publication. It was called "Thunder City's Great Idea"—6000 words. It went first to *Collier's*. No go. Then to *Munsey's*. A week passed. Ten days. The tension was terrific. Then it happened. I was a member of a dancing class at the Terrace; we were being taught the fox-trot by the hotel's new instructor—a slim, dark, diffident and somewhat baffling young man named Arthur Murray, who talked of vague plans for teaching all the world to dance, and the fortune that might be derived therefrom. On a summer's evening when Professor Murray seemed even vaguer than usual, and his small class clumsier than ever, there was a call for me from the office of the *Journal*. A letter had been received from the Frank A. Munsey Company. Not a bulky envelope, either. I asked to have it read over the phone. Here were the contents:

> Dear Sir:
> We have read and can use at $40 your story entitled:
>
> THUNDER CITY'S GREAT IDEA.
>
> If these terms are agreeable kindly advise the writer and check will be sent you the first Wednesday following the date of acceptance.
> Very truly yours,
> THE FRANK A. MUNSEY COMPANY
> By: Robert H. Davis.

It was at that moment, I'm sure, that I decided I'd be in New York, to stay, before the end of 1919. I had immediate visions of writing Thunder City into a film and possibly a play. When I returned to the Palm Room foxtrotters I told Professor Murray that I was giving up Atlanta for New York. His blank look vanished. His eyes brightened. He said that he, too, had reached that same decision.

They didn't give Enrico Caruso a floor at the Georgian-Terrace. Only half a floor. Another half went to Geraldine Farrar. Caruso, Farrar, Gatti, Bori, Alda, Martinelli—they all came South, relaxed, and walked in the sun along Ponce de Leon Avenue. Billy Guard, the famous press man of the Met, and more temperamental than any of his stars, was whisked about town by the Atlanta newsmen covering the opera. Opera wasn't music-page stuff in the three Atlanta dailies; it was front-page news, served with splashing headlines for the city's music-famished, which seemed to be the entire population. Atlanta society swooned with the coming of every April. It went on a cultural carousal and remained in a state of semi-paralysis until the last final note of "Cavalleria Rusticana" or "Pagliacci" had echoed and re-echoed against the granite wall of Stone Mountain. The frenzy was contagious. The society departments did nip-ups in their descriptions of the gowns of the opera-goers, of the teas and receptions and supper dances at the Terrace and at the Piedmont Driving Club. The sons of the socially prominent, quite bored with it all, sat in boxes and sipped with straws from hip flasks. The U. D. C. and the D. A. R., the Elks and the Shrine and the Odd Fellows, and all the descendants of Joel Chandler Harris, forgot their immediate cares for opera-week observance. Seemingly, the only Atlantian who did not suffer a complete loss of poise was an elderly lady named Mrs. Coolidge who lived at the Terrace and who sat imperially, and for endless hours, in a big armchair at the lobby entrance, with all the intruders, from Caruso down, subject to the severity of her glances.

Opera-minded, Atlanta, for one glorious week in every spring; book-minded and theater-minded all the year round. It took pride in the literary prowess of Corra Harris, just as it was later to do in the writing of Margaret Mitchell, and it ranked then, as it does now, as a good book town. It had standing, too, as an amusement center—road shows, stock, screen, vaudeville. The names of Jake Wells, Oscar Oldknow, E. A. Schiller, Richard Herndon and Hugh Cardoza were familiar names in the amusement world of the South. For stock Atlanta generally turned to Lucille LaVerne or Emma Bunting and for touring stars it had Maude Adams in "A Kiss For Cinderella," Jeanne Eagles in "Outcast," Mrs. Fiske, William Hodge, Lew Dockstader, Thomas W. Ross, Tim Murphy, Thomas A. Wise, Wright Lorimer, David Warfield. These players

generally stayed at the Ansley or the old Piedmont. Maude
Adams, with her formidable retinue of female companions,
went to the Piedmont and was traditionally inaccessible.
In Savannah I'd been almost tossed from a moving train
when I sought to interview Miss Adams. In Atlanta she
was a wraith, positively non-existent, and those of us who
had been assigned to track her down were not willing to
admit that she had reached the city at all until the curtain
rose at the old Atlanta on Barrie's delicate little play.

However, the interview that I was denied in Georgia was
to come in later years when she invited me to luncheon at
New York's Colony Club and talked racingly and charm-
ingly of her tour in "The Merchant of Venice," of the old
Empire, of Drew, Frohman and Barrie. In Atlanta, as vir-
tually everywhere outside of New York, dramatic criticism was regarded as merely a pleasant chore, interesting
extra work for those so fortunate as to be assigned to it. A
reporter writing a piece on a play's opening was supposed
to get it out of the way in a hurry so that he'd be available
for regular duties no later, say, than 9 A.M. Ward Greene,
brilliant in his news writing, covered most of the plays.
Angus Perkerson, Sunday magazine editor, served occasionally as critic. Perk, as we knew him, was as able an
editor as you ever saw, but the thought of New York always terrified him. He was a worrier and a man doubtful
of his capacities. He stayed in Atlanta. Greene came north

and began his novel-writing with "Cora Potts." Laurence Stallings, who was to join the Marines and lose a leg, did some reviewing, too; his wage was $12 weekly. He was the best-read man in the Journal office, talked interestingly and incessantly of himself and was as full of confidence as he was of bluster. All of us had turns as play-reviewers. I got about six months of it in one stretch and the only piece I did that seemed to attract attention was a review of "Peg O' My Heart." The play was old by then; a vagrant troupe, barnstorming under dubious sponsorship, brought it to Georgia, where it had been seen several times. In my account of it I said the only member of the cast worth listening to was the dog. The next morning the entire troupe descended in a body upon the *Journal's* city room. Had they encountered a less tactful managing editor than John Paschall they'd probably be there yet.

My New York-before-New Year's campaign had gained momentum by fall. I was getting responses to letters, but no jobs. I sold two more short stories and ran my savings up to $750. I knew the railway fare to New York to the penny, had begun to figure on where we'd live, and had told Jesse Couch of the Georgian-Terrace that we would not want the room beyond Christmas. In late October of 1919 there came a letter from Garet Garrett of the *New York Tribune*. He suggested that I get a copy of the *Tribune*, look it over carefully and tell him what was the matter with it. "Don't hesitate," he said, "to be as harsh as you like." I wrote a thousand-word letter and mailed it with the feeling that it couldn't fail. Two weeks passed. Three. Nothing from Garrett. This was a time when newspapermen worked six and seven days weekly, when the craft had never dreamed of the five-day, forty-hour week and three-weeks' vacation. Few of the *Journal* men took their full two weeks. A week or ten days would go by and they'd either be back at work or hanging around the office. I had my vacation coming to me. I'd go on North and see that fellow Garrett. Go and find out just where I stood. Maybe if that didn't work out there'd be a place somewhere else. I armed myself with "letters," those dread things that have been part of the equipment of all of us bent upon conquest of New York, hopefully courageously and undespairing, no matter how slim the chances and how great the odds. Letters to F.P.A., Grantland Rice, Keats Speed, Jack Tennant, Brisbane, Munsey, Bill Seabrook. Just a trip to New York, I explained to everybody; just to get a look at Broadway for the first time. Maybe I'd see George Cohan and tell him about my play. Or maybe I'd get a chance to meet Dillingham or Morris Gest or Al Woods, who was always buying plays from unknowns and giving them staggering advances. Back in two weeks, I said, and never meaning a word of it. The dark-haired young woman who had been one of the best Latin scholars in the history of Agnes Scott College took me to the Peachtree station. . . . The Southern Railway. . . . Gainesville, Salisbury, N. C., Danville, Va., Lynchburg, and on to Washington and New York. . . . The train was on time. I stepped aboard. I called to her as she stood on the platform, in tears, and told her to begin packing. I knew then that I would not be back.

New York's hotels were jammed. I'd been told they would be but was hardly prepared for the abruptness of the room clerks. I tried four or five hotels in the immediate area of the Pennsylvania Station. "No rooms," they said challengingly. No rooms. No rooms. Finally, at the McAlpin, I did get a mere slit of a room—dark and $4 daily. I looked over my introduction letters, tucked a handful of them into the inside pocket of my coat, and started for Park Row and Nassau Street. I was prepared to make the rounds, going first to the *Tribune*. But that proved to be my first and last stop. It seemed taken for granted that I'd been hired by Garet Garrett. They'd been wondering why it had taken me so long to come North. No, Mr. Garrett wasn't around. But Mr. Macfarland knew all about it. I didn't see Garrett that day. Or the next. Or ever. His connection with the paper ended suddenly and mysteriously. The long line of *Tribune* managing editors, successors to Garrett in a precarious post, began forming on the left.

My wife came North in two weeks, bringing along all our possessions, including $750, an L. C. Smith typewriter, the first act of a play called "The Turtle Dove," and stacks of notes on short stories. We took a room with friends from the South in their Haven Avenue apartment. Haven Avenue was reached via the West Side subway—168th Street station—and the apartment in which the Wilkinsons lived was on the river side. The winter of 1919-20 was one of the coldest in New York's history; zero and sub-zero at times. Forecaster James Henry Scarr's name was forever in print, along with those of Governor Smith, Mayor Hylan, District Attorney Swann, F. H. LaGuardia (Board of Aldermen) and the Rev. Dr. Percy Stickney Grant. From November until early spring New York shivered in the icy winds, wallowed in the snow and slush. The day that I first set foot upon Manhattan the city froze in the paralyzing clutch of one of the winter's coldest weeks. The Haven Avenue apartment, way up there on the margin of the island, was an icebox. The building seemed to overhang the Hudson, irresolutely. It shook under the force of the river gales, and appeared about ready to topple over at any moment. We stood it for a month or so and then moved to a two-room apartment in the Columbia University area—119th Street, furnished and $80 per month. Snug compared with Haven Avenue, but there was no escaping the cold—as severe, I suppose, as that of Atlanta's fall of 1917 when the flu epidemic swept the country and men at Camp Gordon, as at other cantonments, died by thousands.

I did general reporting in my first six months on the *Tribune*, later shifting to the night side and the rewrite desk. The *Tribune* staff of 1919-20 was a big one. Able, too. The blustering Boyden Sparkes was the star man, a fine reporter. Tom Steep, who'd been to China, got important assignments. So did M. Jay Racusin. Ishbel Ross and Emma Bugbee were as good a pair of news-getters as any city editor would ever want. Morris Werner, who was later to write "Barnum" and other biographies, was on obits and grumbled about it. Arthur Folwell came on from the periodical field and put life into the Sunday magazine. The two best writers on the staff, Bob Peck and F. F. Van de Water, were on the night rewrite battery. Peck is today, and has been for twenty-five years, the outstanding rewrite man in America. Heywood Broun was dramatic critic. Phil Mindil was dramatic editor, and an arrogant little man named Fishkind did dramatic notes and some of the second-string reviews. Mindil soon died and Beauvais Fox came on as dramatic editor. Broun, who had been covering baseball only a few years before and who was now establishing a reputation as a play reviewer, was already getting offers to go elsewhere. He was thinking them over.

It was a newsy winter. The nations' coal miners went on

strike. Prohibition, and its running mate, the Eighteenth Amendment, came along; New York's City Hall was a three-ring circus, with Hylan, LaGuardia and Comptroller Craig among the participants. The Prince of Wales, wearing the uniform of a colonel of the Welsh Guards with four rows of ribbons across his chest, came to New York and conquered it. A pretty girl reporter danced with him and was never the same again. He was shown the Woolworth Tower and the Stock Exchange and the East Side and he was welcomed at Old Trinity by Bishop Manning. Munsey, beginning his slaughter of the New York dailies, killed off the *Herald*. Maurice Maeterlinck came to our responsive shores. The names of Rodman Wanamaker and John Mc E. Bowman and Grover Whalen were familiar to all readers of newsprint. The nation's Federal agents, directed by the square-jawed A. Mitchell Palmer, began "Rounding up the Reds." In New York they were arrested by the wagonload, hustled to precinct stations, shipped to Ellis Island and locked in cages, pending deportation. Dempsey was heavyweight champion, Charles F. Murphy was boss of Tammany Hall, and the Cincinnati Reds ruled baseball. There were murmurs about the White Sox, but their story was yet to break. Pussyfoot Johnson was in the news and so were Gompers, Borah, Senator Lodge, Carranza, Lady Astor, Carter Glass, Trotsky, Emma Goldman, Rose Pastor Stokes. Little Billy Dansey was murdered deep in Jersey. Sinclair Lewis published his novel, "Free Air"; "Main Street" was soon to come. And Actors' Equity, which had won a strike, with the theater's great stars parading and with chorus members making speeches from the statue of Nathan Hale, was now planning to do its own producing.

I got top assignments at the *Tribune* after I'd been there a few weeks. I spent a week at Ellis Island during the time the government, absurdly frantic, was spreading its Red dragnet and I was there when the members of the Russian Workers Union, defiant in their cages, went on hunger strike and refused Thanskgiving turkey and plum pudding. New York reporters on general work reported around 1:30 for afternoon assignments; they seldom got more than two. On evenings when there was no night assignment I often found myself free at 8 P.M. and I hurried to Broadway. During that winter I saw Drinkwater's "Abraham Lincoln," Morris Gest's spectacle-play "Aphrodite," Tarkington's "Clarence," Billie Burke in "Caesar's Wife," Wilton Lackaye in "Palmy Days," Ruth Chatterton in "Moonlight and Honeysuckle" and the late James Forbes's "The Famous Mrs. Fair," the final hit of his career, though he kept at his playwriting for another ten years. Henry Miller and Blanche Bates gave their distinguished services to "The Famous Mrs. Fair," but the young Margalo Gillmore gave it drama and vitality. The Broadway of that winter paid its tribute, too, to the glories of the silent films: Alice Joyce, Pauline Frederick, Geraldine Farrar, Gloria Swanson, William S. Hart, Constance Talmadge, Katherine MacDonald. The Capitol billed itself as "the world's largest theater." The Hippodrome, given over to spectacles, was offering "Happy Days." Burlesque reigned at the Columbia. Gatti-Cazazza presided over the Metropolitan and its stars: Caruso, Farrar, Scotti, Martinelli, Amato, Rothier. The concert field claimed John McCormack and Galli-Curci and Emmy Destinn and Tettrazini and Kreisler and Mischa Elman. The dine, wine and dance spots, soon to vanish, included Murray's Roman Gardens, Churchill's, Joel's, the Strand Roof and Reisenweber's up at the Circle. There was merriment in all of them when old Trinity chimed in the year of 1920. And all of it belonged to the mid-Manhattan area of that memorable winter. But it was the theater, the good old spoken stage, the flesh and blood drama, that held first place in my consciousness, that gave New York City its most marketable product. I gorged myself.

The theater was rampant. Fifty-odd attractions held sway. Sometimes twenty, sometimes thirty, plays were available at bargain prices in Gray's basement at 8:20 P.M. How many times I wriggled through that mob! The drama overflowed its midtown boundaries, lapping Broadway's strand as far north as Ninety-sixth Street (Shubert-

Riviera) and extending, in its vast prosperity, all the way to the shoals of Flatbush. It was a day in which the producers were personalities to as great, and even greater, extent than their players. It was a day in which producers actually had money and actually put their own money into their shows. The managerial list was formidable and impressive: Cohan & Harris, William A. Brady, Wagenhals & Kemper, A. H. Woods, Henry W. Savage, George C. Tyler, Winthrop Ames, Ziegfeld, Edgar and Arch Selwyn, Crosby Gaige, Arthur Hopkins, C. B. Dillingham, John Golden and Winchell Smith, the Shuberts, the mighty Abe Erlanger. On the amusement pages of the New York dailies the theaters were advertised in two separate chunks —the Shubert-controlled houses under the heading, "America's foremost theaters and hits, direction of Lee and J. J. Shubert" and the Erlanger houses, in a smaller grouping, labeled "New York's leading theaters and successes." The Shuberts, with their vast empire, were arrogant in their dealings with the newspapers. There was little hesitancy about barring a critic. The threat of disbarment and advertising withdrawal was a weapon always in use. C. P. Greneker, who had succeeded Toxen Worm as general press representative, was given his orders by "Mr. Lee" and Greneker bore down constantly. His peremptory demands for space, photographs and otherwise, were not to be ignored. If a notice of a play was not to the Shuberts'

liking "Mr. Lee" spoke to Greneker and Greneker protested to the offending publication. Many times he was seen
at the *Tribune* building, ominously, mysteriously, and asking not for the managing editor, whoever that happened to
be, but for Mrs. Reid. In later years, with the Shuberts'
properties ever on the increase, and before their decline
was ever predictable, I was assigned to cover a dull musical
piece called "Countess Maritza." It was a second-string
assignment. Greneker's boldness, under his office's prompt-
ings, was such that he asked me to meet him before the
first curtain. He explained that I had an important assignment and that he hoped I would "rise to the occasion." His
exact words. The inference was that if I didn't fully appreciate the show it would be just too bad. I didn't like
"Countess Maritza." Not many people did. I told the office
of the talk with Greneker before I wrote the review. But
Charles Belmont Davis, the dramatic editor and brother
of Richard Harding Davis, counseled caution. He wanted
no quarrel with the Shuberts, with Greneker, with Mrs.
Reid, with Managing Editor Holcombe, with anybody.
He suggested that I give the show something approximat-
ing a rave. I've always regretted the notice I wrote. But
the Shuberts and C. P. Greneker beamed when they read
the *Tribune's* account of "Countess Maritza."

The theatrical managers of that day lived well. They all
spent money freely, particularly those who didn't have it.

They had expensive homes. They took trips. They went to London and to Paris, to California, to Palm Beach, to Hot Springs, to French Lick. They week-ended at the shore. Atlantic City was then the most desirable spot for trying out a play in all America and almost any Saturday afternoon you'd find Al Woods (if he hadn't just sailed), Lee Shubert, George M. Cohan, Sam H. Harris, Martin Herman and George White on the Boardwalk. Ziegfeld indulged himself in Hearstian fashion. He wore the finest shirtings that could be bought, sent thousand-word telegrams of abuse to employes and associates, collected jade elephants, talked long-distance to all the world and maintained a zoo at Hastings-on-Hudson. Al Woods was on the Atlantic when he wasn't at Atlantic City or at the Eltinge Theater, with a Corona Corona in his mouth and his expensively shod feet resting on his desk. He made decisions at 11:30 P.M. to sail on the *Majestic* or the *Berengaria*, leaving at midnight. Why not? Indeed, why not? He had five or six hits running, most of them on the same street, and his road argosies were plentiful and prosperous.

Theaters were going up, up. Two young architects, the brothers Chanin, were looking longingly at Broadway. A young actress named Cornell was soon to startle Broadway with the magic of her playing in a piece called "A Bill of Divorcement." A dramatist named O'Neill, son of an old-school actor, was to give Broadway his first long play, "Beyond the Horizon." A critic named Woollcott was brightening the daily and Sunday *Times* with his emotional prose and had thereby drawn the fire of George Jean Nathan who called him, in the *Smart Set*, the "Seidlitz powder of Times Square." A novelist named Lewis was finishing the biggest job of his life, the writing of "Main Street." And a press agent named Hoffenstein, ex-dramatic critic, was bringing a touch of literature to publicity. His blasting review of Belasco's "Marie Odile" had cost him his job on the *Evening Sun*.

And so came the evening of February 2, the year of Nineteen Hundred and Twenty. Three plays were opening —William J. Hurlbut's "Trimmed in Scarlet," starring Maxine Elliot; "My Golden Girl," which had a Victor Herbert score and "The Night Boat," which was being presented at the Liberty. There was a shortage of reviewers that evening. The dramatic department had asked the day desk for assistance and the day desk, characteristically, had passed the request along to the night desk. Dwight S. Perrin, drumming his fingers on a great stack of unread copy, gave the story about the Rev. Dr. Percy Stickney Grant to Frederick Beecher Edwards (more of this fellow later) and told me I was covering a show. I drew the Liberty Theater and had an evening of good comedy, lively tunes and dancing by the lank Hal Skelly and the fat-legged but agile Louise Groody. My review was all right from the box office angle. I said (brightly, I thought) that "The Night Boat" was certain of a long voyage. But that one assignment was the ruin of me in general news coverage. I decided upon an easier and probably far less satisfying life. My goal was now Broadway and the dramatic department.

I began wondering how it could happen—and when.

## The Early Twenties

THREE YEARS WENT BY. FOUR. I FINALLY ACHIEVED THE
dramatic department, bought a cane, called Al Woods by
his first name, and began covering Broadway. But the
happenings of the intervening years, before I made the
shift from the night desk to the theatrical coop, were
eventful ones for the theater, for the city room, for after-
dark phases of New York life, and must not go unre-
corded. The early twenties, pieced together and assayed,
belong to such a personal chronicle as this is to be.

Careers were taking shape. Playwrights were in the
making. Players, too. An old and spectacular order of
theatrical managers was passing; giants of play production
were disappearing fast, quitting or dying off, and generally with little in worldly possessions to show for their
labors. Broadway's night-life map was being made over.
Speakeasies, the ornate and dingy, the reputable and low-
down, took up operations in midtown Manhattan. The
Broadway area, shorn of its legendary glamour spots,
began to lose caste. The playhouses remained, but the
after-theater drift of night-prowlers was to the East. Many

29

of those associated with the drinking establishments of prohibition years are now in jail or in their graves. The era developed, however, several super hosts—and astute business men along with it—who established themselves during the Twenties and increased their followings in the Thirties. Jack Kriendler (Vienna born) and Charlie Berns moved from Forty-ninth to Fifty-second and there, at No. 21, opened what is probably the most interesting and most spectacularly successful bar-club-restaurant in all America. John Perona, once a bus-boy, came along with El Morocco, zebra stripes and a more or less exclusive clientele. Sherman Billingsley, a genial Oklahoman, drew hordes to his Stork Club during prohibition and he took Repeal in stride. Vincent Sardi, from the north of Italy, quit his original stand in Forty-fourth Street and moved to his present quarters, just one hundred feet to the east, and with the walls patiently bearing caricatures of all the celebrities (dubious rating in most cases) who ever set foot in the place. Tony Soma, who was once Caruso's floor waiter at the old Hotel Knickerbocker, packed a Forty-ninth Street basement (at $1 a drink) during peephole days, and continued his prosperity in Fifty-second. Jack Bleeck, from out of St. Louis, established Ye Olde Grille—steaks and chops and liquor if they knew you—at Fortieth Street and Seventh Avenue in the early Twenties. He now presides, and mellowly, over the Artists and Writers Restaurant, alongside the *Herald Tribune* in Fortieth Street, and there members of the staff, prominent and otherwise, become engaged nightly in a fascinating and destructive pastime called the match game. Ogden Reid doesn't play matches but he does his drinking at Bleeck's. He no longer keeps his cabs waiting all night as he used to do in Nassau Street. He would sleep until daybreak in a chair in his office and his driver, parked at the curb, would doze at the wheel, with the meter ticking away merrily, hour upon hour.

Those early Twenties witnessed the sure, steady strides of Eugene O'Neill. They saw the rise of Kaufman & Connelly as a playwriting team; the development of the Theater Guild as the theater's foremost producing organization; the projection of John Barrymore to the status of First Actor; the coming to New York of Percy Hammond, and the presentation of such memorable drama as "Loyalties," "Anna Christie," "Rain" and "What Price Glory." Two fine actresses of the era, Jeanne Eagels and Emily Stevens, both of whom were to die all too soon, were just rising to the fullness of their powers. Jeanne Eagels gave her truly magnificent performance as Sadie Thompson and Emily Stevens distinguished herself in "Fata Morgana" and later as Hedda Gabler. Katharine Cornell and Helen Hayes came along as certainties for future greatness. The late Holbrook Blinn was at the top of his profession, just then gaining, seemingly, recognition as the consummate artist that he had been through the years. Alfred Lunt revealed talent and exuberance for the theater in his playing in Booth Tarkington's "Clarence." Tallulah Bankhead, discouraged by her Broadway adventures, although she was always getting jobs, decided to try her luck in another street, another town, another country. She borrowed $1,000 from General Coleman Dupont, was given a gay farewell party at the old Waldorf and took a boat for England. Some of the older players, their careers closing, drifted into the rôles of lookers-on. John Drew lolled at the Players'. David Warfield was preparing to quit. Henry Miller, William Faversham, Otis Skinner, William Gillette—they all were tired. Maxine Elliott went to the Mediterranean—to stay. Mrs. Fiske, the indomitable, kept on, active until her death. Eleanor Robson had left the theater and so had Mary Mannering, Viola Allen, Julia Marlowe, Edna May, Marie Doro, Rose Stahl. Maude Adams was at Lake Ronkonkoma and in a retirement from which she was to emerge, perhaps unwisely, in the fall of 1931.

A new order of playwrights, too, was replacing the old. Augustus Thomas, Eugene Walter, George Broadhurst, Thompson Buchanan, James Forbes, Avery Hopwood—their day was done. Rachel Crothers remained an exception. She'll go on forever. Owen Davis will be writing plays so long as he can lift a pencil. But the new surge of talent, the realists, revoltists, experimenters, was on its way. Led by O'Neill, the group included Maxwell Anderson, George S. Kaufman, Sidney Howard, Marc Connelly, Philip Barry, Zona Gale, Zoe Akins, George Kelly, Lula Vollmer, Ben Hecht, Sam Behrman. O'Neill followed his "Beyond the Horizon" with his powerful "Anna Christie" and his "Strange Interlude" was not far away. Maxwell Anderson, with the presentation of "What Price Glory" (written in collaboration with Laurence Stallings), quit his $150-a-week editorial-writing job on the old *World* to give full time to the theater. George S. Kaufman hung on warily at the *Times*, holding his job as dramatic editor and second-string reviewer until his hits had piled up on him. George Kelly, who now appears to have completely lost interest, came along with three successes in a row. Elmer Rice fulfilled the promise of his playwriting youth—we don't forget "On Trial"—and became one of the boldest of them all in the use of new dramatic forms. The New York theater of the early and mid-Twenties was not without aid from London, best represented by Galsworthy, Maugham and Lonsdale. Of all the old-school playwrights of Broadway it was Winchell Smith who seemed best at readjustment. His hit-formula of the "Fortune Hunter"—"Turn to the Right"—"Lightnin' " era was worn out. But Billy Smith, adapting himself to the new demands, forms and trends, held his place as a play-fixer, script counselor and director with an amazing instinct for dramatic values. I've always felt that his feel for the theater could have made him as facile with "Hamlet" as with "The First Year." He took a great fortune out of the theater and he earned every penny of it. Billy Smith, the actors will tell you, was the stage director of our time.

Broadway, before the Twenties were half gone, had sixty or so theaters available for legitimate production. And yet there was a cry for more playhouses, the theater's demand for living space! So the Chanins came along and put up one, two, three, four, five! And the realty domain of Lee and J. J. Shubert, two of the three restless brothers who came down from Syracuse just before the turn of the century, was ever spreading.

I shifted to the Night Side in the spring of 1920, got a pay increase from $50 to $60 weekly, sat with Bob Peck and F. F. Van de Water on the rewrite battery, and worked directly under Dwight S. Perrin and B. O. Mc-Anney. On my night off—newspapermen in that pre-Guild era got one day off a week and were quite blissful about it—I went to the theater, occasionally covering a show. But a week never passed in which I didn't see at least one Broadway play. Generally two, and always in

THE EARLY TWENTIES 35

the balcony or second balcony and paying my way. My night off and the première of David Belasco's revival of "The Easiest Way," with Frances Starr as Laura Murdock, the late Joseph Kilgour in his original rôle of the Wall Street man, and Robert Kelly (he was later to create the rôle of the Rev. Davidson in "Rain") as the Westerner who struck gold, fell upon the same day. This was one of the first first-nights that Noel Coward, newly arrived from London, and eager and frightened, attended in New York. And on that evening, as he has recounted, he met Alexander Woollcott, being introduced by Beatrice Kaufman. Such was the beginning of a friendship that has endured, incredibly enough, ever since. Years later when Woollcott decided he wanted to sell his co-operative East River apartment, he found a ready purchaser in Coward, probably the most versatile and sought-after man of the theater that England has ever sent to our susceptible metropolis.

I saw little of New York during the months of Night Side labors. City Hall Park, Broadway for weekly play-going, Morningside Heights and West Side subway formed my world. I'd burrow below the street level at 116th Street and clamber up for air six miles to the south, at Park Place. Night after night, month after month. My rewrite hours shifted frequently—5 P.M. to 1 A.M., or 6 to 2 or 8 to 4. New York City is, of course, a city comprising a thousand-odd compact little cities, all smug within their borders; neighborhoods with the villagey touch, precincts within precincts, boroughs within boroughs, and each with its own feuds and fellowships, its own characters and characteristics and its own more or less permanent populations. I got to know Amsterdam Avenue as I was to know Broadway. Cobble-stoned Amsterdam Avenue and its multitudinous tea rooms, its frumpy-looking summer students, its young and old in tennis whites and carrying racquets, its dingy apartment houses with young women seeking their B.A.'s living four in a room, and its rattling trolleys bouncing at a fearful clip down that steep hill to 125th Street.

I worked fiercely in my spare time, afternoons on Morningside Heights and after midnight at my rewrite desk when the night's grind eased up. The rewrite job was often strenuous, particularly so when either Peck or Van de Water had a night off. They both handled a terrific lot of copy. Perrin and McAnney piled many pieces done by the assignment men into the rewrite basket. All the stars of the staff achieved that basket sooner or later. Wilbur Forrest, who had had foreign correspondence experience and whose vague present-day status is something of a cross between Ogden Reid's assistant and shadow, was a steady customer. Perrin wouldn't accept "involved" leads and Forrest was forever writing them.

It appeared to be his duty to interpret any despatch concerning anything that happened in any part of the world
to the east of Newfoundland. Sparkes, who was to become a regular contributor to the *Saturday Evening Post*
and other publications, was often on the verge of giving
a personal thrashing to any man who touched his stuff.
The political experts, Charles White and Dennis Tilden
Lynch, accepted rewriting as a matter of routine. It happened pretty regularly to both. Some staff members protested feebly to the day desk, others kept quiet and
brooded, but no one ever questioned or challenged the
competence of the Night Side overhaulers, Peck & Van de
Water. I sold several short pieces to minor magazines,
a few items to *Life* and *Judge* and got an "almost acceptance" from the *Saturday Evening Post*—it was signed by
T. B. Costain—on a story called "Mr. Doom Gets A Letter," all about an old fellow who'd worked nearly all his
life in a small-town post-office without having received
so much as a post card. I contributed a feature called "This
Town of Ours," flash impressions of New York, to the
*Tribune's* Sunday magazine. It was done in the dot, dot,
dot manner, a form of writing which was to be taken up
by column writers, tabloid and otherwise, from one end
of the country to the other. I also started a New York
letter, selling it to a group of Southern dailies, and finished
the play called "The Turtle Dove." Nobody ever bought

"The Turtle Dove." It was probably pretty terrible. It
received, however, a good deal of attention in a prize play
contest started by the *Morning Telegraph*. I didn't really
give up on "The Turtle Dove" until I went to Winchell
Smith's place at Farmington, Conn. He suggested that I
read the script to him. He'd read many of his own plays
to managers. He got a hearty acceptance of "The Fortune Hunter" from George M. Cohan by reading the
first act in a hotel room in Buffalo. So, in the midnight
quiet of his study in the beautiful home he had built on
the outskirts of Hartford, I read Act One. And then he
said, as gently as possible, that perhaps it would be just
as well not to go on. He poured the Scotch and told me
why.

There was a copy reader on the *Tribune* named Fitzgerald. We called him Fitz and he had rating as one of
the best. He knew his job. He wrote headlines swiftly
and he wrote them well and he was the never-sleep wonder of his time. He worked a full day shift on the *Brooklyn Times*, which he considered his job "on the side,"
and put in an eight-hour shift, beginning at 6 P.M., at the
*Tribune*. It would have been quite within character, and
certainly within his limitless endurance, for him to have
hired out for the lobster trick on a morning paper in
Newark. Well, Fitz came into the *Tribune* one evening
pretty excited. He charged over to my desk. There was

a vacancy on the *Brooklyn Times*. Rewrite. The rewrite staff, consisting of exactly one man, had been fired. They wanted somebody from Manhattan. He'd told them about me. Swell chance, urged Fitz, to pick up an extra $55 weekly and only four hours a day! But when, I wondered, would I ever sleep. Hell, argued Fitz, I was generally off at 1 A.M., wasn't I? And how much sleep did I want, for God's sake? And what did I do with my mornings any-way?

I took the job in Brooklyn. I kept at it off and on for five years and for a time my newspaper schedule, as I now remember it, ran like this: *Brooklyn Times*, 9 A.M. to 1 P.M.; Broadway and Morningside Heights, 2 P.M. to 5 P.M.; *Tribune* rewrite, 6 P.M. to 1 or 2 A.M. There were evenings when I was so weary it was all I could do to get across City Hall Park and fall into a bunk at the baths of the Woolworth Building, only ten minutes or so from Atlantic Avenue and the *Brooklyn Times*. In those days I seemed to have endless vitality (but nothing approxi-mating that of Copy Reader Fitzgerald) and I really liked the Brooklyn rewrite, once I ever got there. Most of the local front page stuff came to my desk. Lester Rice, who turned to sports writing, was my first Brooklyn city editor; Walter Lister, now on the city desk of the *New York Post*, was next, and then came the gruff Bill Wil-liams. I enjoyed talks in rewrite lulls with Lister, and with

John Harmon, who was editor of the *Times* and who was forever talking of Broadway first nights and Brooklyn politics. I'd give up the Brooklyn slaving every now and then, swearing never to return, but I'd always go back, and it so happened that I was doing a siege of across-the-river rewrite when my *Tribune* job suddenly blew up on an evening in the fall of 1926.

The most precarious of all newspaper jobs, for a time, was the managing-editorship of the *Tribune*. Garet Garrett vanished and along came George Smith, brought over from the Munsey camp. Here was the steadying, conservative, phlegmatic executive needed for the spot, the Reids decided. George Smith died. And then Bill McGeehan, to his complete bewilderment, was yanked out of the sports department and made the big boss. McGeehan, an able sports commentator, was in a daze as a managing editor. He fully realized it. When the Reids finally gave up on Bill they went all the way to Chicago for their next victim: Julian Mason, who'd been to Yale, who used elegant cigarette holders and who had a way of dropping into the office at midnight in a white tie, with a group of ladies and gentlemen in tow. Mason was cold, inhuman and sly. He was cordially disliked by the staff. When the time came for his eventual departure—it was quite as sudden as Garet Garrett's had been—he experienced no inconvenience. He calmly stepped into another job, the editorship of the *Evening Post*. He sent for Ralph Renaud, then on the *World*, and made him managing editor. Renaud was with the *Tribune* for some years. A fellow who had a definite driving quality and certain capabilities. In his relaxed moments he was happiest when telling dirty stories, and he did it rather well. When not so engaged he was playing his other rôle, that of the bully of the Night Side. There never was a man surer in his news judgments than Renaud—that is, sure until the first edition of the *Times* came in. Then his bellowings would shake the city room. A quick glance at the *Times* front page and the *Tribune's* "A" on "Strike" would shrink to a "B" for the make-over; the "B" on "Reds" would jump to an "A" and lead the page. And so it went. These self-reversals at midnight gave many a chuckle to Perrin or Van de Water or McAnney or Ira Crist or whoever happened to be sitting in as night city editor. Renaud is now with the *Times*. Julian Mason has been out of newspaper work since leaving the *Post*.

The *Tribune* bought the *Herald* from Frank A. Munsey in March of 1924 and became the *Herald Tribune*. It had already moved into the new plant in West Fortieth Street. The Reids by now were running out of managing editors and with the exit of Mason it became necessary, once more, to find a man for the m.e.'s pen. This time the Reids, probably with the assent of Geoffrey Parsons, chief editorial writer, decided again upon a member of the staff—Armistead Holcombe, the night editor. Holcombe was white-haired, easy-going, non-resisting, un-eventful. He held on for a time. Eventually he, too, was fired. He went to Maryland, took over a small-town weekly, and was happy to be out of New York. But he died within a year or so. Grafton Wilcox, an erstwhile political writer, was the next in line, the sixth managing editor in seven years. He apparently has done a good job. He's held the post continuously ever since.

It was during the régime of Julian Mason that one Frederick Beecher Edwards came into a measure of re-nown. A Canadian, Edwards, with years of experience in Montreal and Halifax. Rather spare of frame, lackadaisi-cal, and never hesitant about speaking his mind. He was a glib writer and effortless in his work. It got to be known around the city room when the *Tribune* was downtown that I'd sold a few short stories. Ishbel Ross had notions that she might like to do novels some day. Boyden Sparkes had never written a line for a magazine but thought he might try. Edwards and I sat side by side on rewrite and he said, well, short-story writing looked easy, and what the hell? Why not? He needed some money and he had a comic idea. And so, in his own casual way, and in a week or so of spare-time writing at his desk, he turned out a 7,500-word story and sent it to the *Saturday Evening*

*Post.* He heard from it within ten days. Yes, they liked "Thank-You-Please Perkins." They'd take it at $400. And wouldn't he let them sell some more of his stories? Freddie read the note without batting an eye, went into a booth and telephoned his wife. They were living in a gloomy flat on the upper West Side. "Oh, thank God," cried Mrs. Edwards, "now I can have some clothes, some clothes!" Edwards was the only man in the city room who had sold a piece of fiction to the *Post* and he automatically became something of an office hero. But an even greater triumph awaited him. The *Tribune* staff was given to frequent get-togethers. There was a dinner at Delmonico's, and a brawl in Hoboken. When Mason was in the managing editor's chair Keen's chop house in Forty-fourth Street was decided upon as an excellent spot for a festive evening. But this dinner was unlike any that had gone before. Verbal fireworks supplied the drama. The transient Mason, white-tied and perfection itself, attended and he made a speech. He may not have intended to put it as he did, but before he'd finished he was facing a resentful and mutinous roomful. He said, in effect, that everybody present was getting all the pay they deserved and that he could buy the likes of 'em in the open market. Then Edwards got up. He replied calmly, persuasively and yet bitingly, and put Mason in his place, which was anywhere at that moment except Keen's in Forty-fourth

Street. Ogden Reid rose and backed up Edwards. Good for Oggie! Two days later Edwards was given a watch as a tribute from the staff and a short time later Mason announced that Mr. Edwards was the new city editor. He eventually went back to Montreal, as he'd always said he would. The last time I saw him, in the lobby of the Mount Royal Hotel, he was telling the time by a handsome gold watch, affectionately engraved.

Now, in the meantime, there'd been changes in the drama department. The *World*, the most forceful of the New York dailies, was making a strong staff stronger. It had wanted Broun and it got him. The *Tribune* sent to Chicago's Loop for Percy Hammond. It was a smart move. Hammond became a fixture in New York and served as critic until his death sixteen years later.

I was on night rewrite when I beheld Percy Hammond, fussing over the proofs of his first review in the East. It was an account of a trivial piece called "Sonya," with Violet Heming and Otto Kruger. We talked that night and had many after-midnight sessions in succeeding years. He liked the Type and Point Club, a dingy speakeasy that got the *Tribune's* trade before Jack Bleeck's vogue set in. Once his review was done, he was in a mood for marching. He liked doing the town—the Hotsy Totsy, Texas Guinan's, the Chez Florence, Barney Gallant's, Harlem. Anywhere. And everywhere. He seldom bothered to bring

any money along and was as vague in his check-grabbing
and his taxi-paying as Jed Harris has been known to be.
But he was an enchanting conversationalist and particularly so when he was talking of his fancied persecutors,
which was practically all the time. Percy, as all the town
instantly called him, nurtured his hostilities. He resented
his aisle-seat colleagues in his first few months here and he
had the feeling that they resented him. But through all
the years I heard only praise, and lavish praise, for Percy
from his fellow first-nighters. Percy was a brooder. He
enjoyed his frettings and his whinings. They'd hated him
in Chicago, he often told me. His competitive critics and
his immediate associates. The New York critics—Woollcott, Broun, Mantle, Darnton—they didn't like him and
he'd give you the reasons why. His own dramatic department offered no co-operation whatever. Even Watts,
whom he really liked and who was to succeed him, was out
to ruin him. And the Shuberts were planning to bar him
from the theaters of the land. He never excluded himself
from his own incisive deprecations and he often said that if
gin and senility didn't get him the Shuberts would. Percy
Hammond, flabby and beet-complexioned, wrote many
brilliant reviews of New York plays. His pieces, when
read over the morning coffee, seemed to be blissful, skim-
ming, effortless prose. But there never was a critic who
worked more laboriously, so slavishly for word choices,

and to whom composition represented so much blood-sweat. His adjectives, often so exquisitely apt, came the hard way. He often caught editions at the very last minute—he frequently missed them—and when he was done with a review he was a man who'd been through a great ordeal and who needed a quick drink. He generally got it.

It was a time when Frank A. Munsey had all newspaperdom jumpy. No one knew just where he'd strike next. Long before he had bought the *New York Press* to support Theodore Roosevelt's Bull Moose candidacy and the *Press* was now but a dim memory. He bought the *Telegram* in 1920 and merged it in 1924 with the *Evening Mail*, which he had acquired from Henry L. Stoddard. The *Mail* disappeared and so did the *Globe*, which he acquired in 1923. The fewer the papers the fewer the dramatic critics and there was a general shifting of reviewers during the height of Munsey's buying and selling and slaughtering. No critic was sure just where he'd land, if he'd land at all. Burns Mantle's spot was safe because the *Daily News*, New York's first successful tabloid, established in 1919 by Captain Joe Patterson and the Patterson-McCormick clan of Chicago, was booming. Hammond had security with the purchase of the *Herald* by the Reids. Woollcott, who had been hired away from the *Times* by Munsey for service on the *Herald* and subsequently *The Sun*, later went to the *World*. He eventually gave up daily criticism for good and

was succeeded on the *World* by Robert Littel. Gilbert
Gabriel was transferred from the *Telegram* to *The Sun* as
Woollcott's successor. Kenneth Macgowan and James
Craig, reviewing for the *Globe* and *Mail* respectively, retired from the reviewing field with the disappearance of
these papers. There was no longer a critic's job for Littel
when the *World* vanished, nor for Gilbert Gabriel, with
the elimination of the *American*.

I was assistant night city editor when the *Tribune*
moved from Nassau Street to Fortieth. McAnney was on
the night desk. Perrin, who had gone to the *Herald*, returned with the merger and later became city editor. Van
de Water had gone. Sparkes was soon to leave. Also Steep.
Racusin, a good reporter, was being pushed more and more
into the rôle of private detective. Peck remained No. 1
man of the rewrite staff. I didn't like desk work but had
the feeling that the dramatic department opening would
come along at any minute. The assistant night city editorship was a lazy man's routine under the system prevailing
in the *Tribune* office at the time. The rewrite men wrote
the copy and the night city editor passed on it. There was
little for the assistant to do except to talk to the district
reporters and read the stuff of the *City News* and *Standard
News* as it flowed from the tickers. During those long
evenings I got to thinking about a play about newspapermen. A newspaper play that would have the true flavor

and the true characters. No romantic nonsense. Something
that would transfer the city room to the stage for the first
time. Why not just such a city room as now lay before
me? No commotion. No screaming for copy boys. No
goings-on such as we'd been accustomed to seeing in the
films. But a piece that would be recognizably true as to
locale and as to character. Indeed, why not? Such reveries
on that night desk led to a play called "Gentlemen of the
Press" and to a première at Henry Miller's Theater, after
a week's run in Atlantic City, some four years later.

We decided—my pretty Georgia-born wife and I—that
we'd been on Morningside Heights long enough and we
moved to that charming row of houses, Pomander Walk,
west of Broadway, and running through from Ninety-
fourth to Ninety-fifth Street. We'd given many parties at
the Amsterdam Avenue apartment, and all of them at-
tracted mobs. Newspaper people came in droves. And they
came to Pomander Walk, along with people of the theater.
Percy Hammond was a frequent caller at the Walk. Emily
Stevens, playing in "Fata Morgana" at the Shubert Riviera
just around the corner, dropped in for tea. Helen Menken
came up several times. So did Louis Wolheim, triumphant
as Captain Flagg in "What Price Glory." Richard Watts,
shy, pink-faced and given to politeness in those days, was
always a welcome guest. Herbert Stothart, who'd done
songs for "Rose-Marie," and his wife Dorothy, who later

killed herself. Arthur Kober came and Willard Keefe, Channing Pollock, Sammy Shipman, and Harry Kline, who was one of my first friends in the Broadway district, and who did so much to help me with my contacts and to encourage me in my writing.

And then came the night when Percy Hammond, over his twelfth cup of coffee—I think Louis Wolheim had a like number—said that I could probably expect to get into the dramatic department most any day. There was ill-feeling between Percy and Frank Vreeland, who was doing the theater news and second-string reviews. Percy figured it might develop any minute into actual violence. They had disliked each other from the very beginning and the hostility was getting stronger all the time. Vreeland resigned. I went to Julian Mason and asked for the job. We hadn't had a word together in a year. He received me with his customary frigidity but as I talked—it was only the second time we'd ever talked—he listened. When I finished he said, "Well, I'll see." That was all. He sent a note to Percy Hammond who must have given his approval. Two days later Dwight Perrin told me to report for duty in the dramatic department. His words at the time have stayed in my memory.

"Go ahead," he said, "because it's what you want to do, and you know how to do it. But I hate to see you do it. It will be the ruin of a good newspaperman. And remember, being in that department is like being managing editor. It's the open door off the *Tribune*."

Reporters were carrying canes and I brought mine. I took over the Broadway beat. The Broadway picture at the moment was like this:

The drama reporters met daily in the Eltinge Theater office of Martin Herman, great friend of the newsmen and the most outspoken showman of his time.

The Hotsy Totsy and the Chez Florence were the most congested of the night spots.

Producers lunched in the Hunting Room of the Astor. The Round Table sessions were on at the Algonquin. Sammy Shipman, the most industrious of the dramatists, received daily in offices in the *Times* Building.

Belasco lived at the Gladstone, and went regularly to Childs. George M. Cohan lived at the Savoy-Plaza (and the Polo Grounds). Wagenhals & Kemper, colorful showmen, were in the Astor Theater Building.

Theater people were discovering the East River. Theatrical and literary sets gathered nightly at Tony's, where practically everybody had the signing privilege.

John Drew frequented the Players. Charles Dillingham, dressed like the dandy that he was, called daily at the New Amsterdam to see A. L. Erlanger, who was only a little less powerful than God.

Oliver Morosco, successful showman, and acrobat on the side, was on his way out. Lenore Ulric was in the picture as a Belasco star. Horace Liveright was neglecting book publishing for play producing.

Walter Kingsley, who had been with the Palace, was soon to join Ziegfeld. Other press agents were Wells Hawks, David Wallace, C. P. Greneker, Frances Reid, Jim Peede, Elbert Severance, Joe Drum.

Jed Harris, a road press agent, was soon to go into producing. Miriam Hopkins was probably the most sought-after ingénue of the moment. Fred Astaire was a hoofer and a minor comic. Kay Francis was in the back room at Tony's. Nobody had ever heard of Myrna Loy.

Ziegfeld, living like the richest man on earth, paraded in Forty-second Street. So did Woods, Aarons & Freedley, Sam Harris, Gaige, the Selwyns, Bickerton, Erlanger, Tyler, Lewis & Gordon.

The *Theater Magazine*, soon to expire, reported the drama. So did *Variety* (Sime Silverman). The *Green Book* and *The Clipper* had passed on.

The Mayfair Club drew the stars to the Ritz Saturday evenings. Chamberlain Brown was the busiest agent and his offices were full of great yellow cats and job-hunting professionals.

Texas Guinan was the queen of night life. Harriette Underhill was the No. 1 film critic. Catherine Dale Owen, Olive Tell, Marion Coakley (and some of the Ziegfeld girls) continued their reign as town beauties.

Walter Winchell was getting started. The Shuberts

parked their cars in Shubert Alley. And nobody had ever heard of Rudy Vallee or Gary Cooper or Clark Gable or even Darryl Zanuck.

And on into the Twenties, second half. . . . Julian Mason was out at the *Tribune* and Holcombe was in. Harriette Underhill, the *Tribune's* motion picture critic, died and Richard Watts, Jr. got the job. Miss Underhill, a semi-invalid for years, had stayed alive by her sheer unwillingness to quit living. I did some of the second-string reviewing; so did Charles Belmont Davis, Watts and, later, Arthur Ruhl. George S. Kaufman, Alison Smith and Quinn Martin were among the town's second-stringers. Managing Editor Holcombe knew little of the theater and cared little for it. When the celebrated "Show Boat" (my notion of the finest musical show in all Broadway's history) came along Watts drew the assignment, Percy electing to cover Philip Barry's "Paris Bound," which was starting the same evening. The "Show Boat" première was sensational. Its success was a certainty after the curtain had been up ten minutes. Watts encountered Holcombe between acts and asked the managing editor what he thought of it. Holcombe dismissed it in three words: "Too many niggers."

I liked the Broadway news-getting job, even under the conditions that existed at the *Tribune*. I made the Broadway rounds afternoons and went to shows in the evenings. The other news-getters included Wells Root of the *World*,

Herman Mankiewicz of the *Times*, Leo Marsh of the *Telegraph*, Jack Pulaski of *Variety*, Bide Dudley of the *Evening World* and, of course, Zolotow of the *Times*. The relentless Zolotow, who has been in the dramatic department of the *Times* since 1921 and an employe of that newspaper since before the war. As a sideline he publishes the *Advance Theatrical Guide*, which comes out weekly and whose subscribers, at $30 a year, include managers, agents and the dramatic departments of the New York dailies. Sam is a digger, knows all the news sources, has the private telephone numbers of nearly everybody in show business, and because of the severity of his cross-examinations had come to be known among the patient showmen as Detective Sergeant Zolotow. All of us went unfailingly to the Eltinge Theater to see Martin Herman. That was headquarters. The Selwyn Theater building was a good news spot. So was the New Amsterdam Theater building. And we all called pretty regularly upon Sam H. Harris, Brock Pemberton, Gus Pitou, C. P. Greneker, Harry Kline, Walter Kingsley and George C. Tyler. Tyler, sitting at an old rolltop desk, was always excellent copy. I set eyes on Erlanger only three or four times. I worked hard for my news beats. My by-line column appeared Sundays and I sought each week to present a mass of exclusive material. My contacts were steadily increasing. I knew the Broadway job and all the people and I liked it tremendously yet

I realized, even from the beginning, that there was no permanence in my assignment—certainly not on the *Herald Tribune*. Holcombe was not interested in the dramatic department. Percy Hammond fancied a breach between himself and the department. He talked constantly of "no co-operation." Charles Belmont Davis had no authority. The "Please-the-Shuberts" policy was ever in evidence. It was not a happy department. Nobody really ran it. It ran itself as best it could.

The New York dailies weren't then so free with space for theatricals as they are today. Agate type was considered sufficient and even eloquent for items of the drama. The *Herald Tribune* gave space grudgingly for news notes. The *Times* buried the daily routine. Only the *World* used an approximation of the big, blown-up theater news columns that are now in evidence. Only Watts, of all our department members, had no complaint about the *Tribune* set-up. He saw no reason why he shouldn't stay on the *Tribune* forever and live to the age of J. Ranken Towse, who died at a mere eighty-eight. Percy, over his third drink, would never fail to talk of an early demise. Davis was a sick man and knew it. Dwight Perrin, with a real fondness for the theater, knew of the state of affairs in the dramatic coop but he had matters of his own on his mind; he was leaving for the prairies to take a better job with the *St. Louis Post Dispatch*. Along in the summer of 1926 I sensed a general blow-up and, as an emergency step, phoned the *Brooklyn Times* and got my old job back. I again worked the double shift. It was now far easier with one instead of two stretches at the rewrite desk.

It was Miss Phelps, who'd served as secretary to the whole parade of *Tribune* managing editors—Garrett, Smith, McGeehan, Mason and Holcombe—who came to the railing of the drama pen several months later. It was around 6 P.M. She said: "Mr. Holcombe would like to see you after dinner, about 9 o'clock." Just said it, and walked away.

Well, I knew. That was the finish. I was fired. It was something, I'd always thought, that should happen at least once to everybody. Fired. I made a thousand plans as I waited for the three hours to pass. Holcombe had great difficulty in finding his words. He said: "I'm having to ask for your resignation. . . . We have decided to bring the drama department up to the efficiency of the other departments of the paper and we want a general reorganization. We're putting in a new dramatic editor. Mr. Davis is going South for his health. . . . Personally I liked your work. But there's nothing else open in the office except a place on the desk and I don't suppose . . ."

When I got off the I.R.T. express at Atlantic Avenue at 8:55 the next morning—it was a Saturday—my step was lighter than it had been in years. What I'd been expecting all along had happened. I now realized that my association with the *Herald Tribune* should have ended long before. I never got to know George Smith. I admired McGeehan as a sports writer but never as an executive. I shared the staff's general hostility for Mason and did not feel that Holcombe even approached the stature of a managing editor. All of us seemed to know, as he must have known, that he was in the rôle only temporarily. And now, as I walked along Atlantic Avenue, I felt rid of a great burden. My Manhattan job was gone, but I had my Brooklyn job and all my Broadway contacts. I knew stars, managers, playwrights. I had my news sources and I intended to stay in the Broadway field.

I'd always been fast on the rewrite desk. A rewrite man has to be if he's any account. But on this particular Saturday morning I believe I was faster than ever. At noon, with everything cleaned up and with the Borough of Brooklyn in one of its quiet moments, the laconic Bill Williams turned, flung up an arm, and said "Go home." But I was expecting a caller. Soon the elevator paused at the City Room level and out popped Miriam Hopkins. She swept toward my desk and the *Brooklyn Times* stopped dead in its tracks. She was then playing the best rôle of her career to date, Sondra in "An American Tragedy," which the late Horace Liveright put on at the Longacre. I'd assisted her in getting the job and she has ever been a person to show her friendship in an emergency. I'd phoned her and we were to meet at Tony's. But she came to Brooklyn. We went to a lunch stand around the corner, sat for an hour, and talked it over.

I was living at the Algonquin. Alexander Woollcott was in the lobby when I returned from Brooklyn. He said that he'd speak to Gilbert Gabriel for me (and he did). I made several quick phone calls. Leo March said yes, there was a spot for me on the *Telegraph* and I could start immediately. My friend Fitzgerald, the Man Who Never Sleeps, was then on the *New York American*, full-time. Sure, he said. There was a rewrite job open at $90. When could I start? And there were three or four other possibilities for immediate connections, two of them out of town. But I wouldn't consider leaving New York. The man for whom I really wanted to work was Keats Speed of the *Sun*. It had been in my mind since I heard legends of him in Atlanta. So I wrote Gabriel, the *Sun's* dramatic critic. Four days later I joined the staff, gave up Brooklyn rewrite, and began the daily column on the theater page, "Broadway After Dark." And in the meantime, the *Herald Tribune* had given the dramatic editorship to a staff man, George Goldsmith. He held it for a year. Then he, too, was fired. Charles Belmont Davis died in the mountains of North Carolina. Arthur Folwell was shifted to *Tribune's* drama desk. He is there today.

I was happy at the *Sun* from the beginning. There you work for just one man, who is the absolute boss. His name is Speed.

Things began happening to me and for me. I wrote and sold a play. I sold scripts and myself to Hollywood. I took my column on tour, writing it from more than fifty countries. And I explored America. Once I had joined the *Sun* I became aware that all that had gone before was but a prelude. My career in New York really began when I reported at 280 Broadway in November of 1926.

## Actors and Actresses

THE REV. NORMAN DAVID MOREHOUSE, MY GRANDFATHER, blasted the devil in the drowsy little towns of South Georgia. He must have had all the tricks and the full repertoire of the circuit rider and from him I undoubtedly inherited yearnings for theatricals. Before ever even thinking of reportorial work I considered the possibilities of a whole series of careers, but with the stage always uppermost in mind. I was told that I should try to write, not act. And that if I didn't write I should develop what appeared to be a talent for painting. For several years, off and on, I'd gone in for art—charcoal, pen and ink, pastel, oil. But I now suspect that most of us were in Miss Julia Boyle's classes solely because of the desire to stay forever in her presence. She was disconcertingly pretty. An audacious nose, lovely mouth and sweeping pompadour. She could have stepped directly from any of the many drawings by Charles Dana Gibson that covered the walls of her big house.

When I did begin to wonder about the newspaper business I had the feeling that reporting would be only a temporary occupation, something that might do for a time and that might aid me, in one way and another, to reach my goal, the theater. My duties with the Minor Stock Company, our amateur producing organization, were endless. I wrote and acted and directed and managed and did all the bookings. The Minor Stock Company, like the jugglers and trombone players and wire-walkers who proclaim their talents in the classified ads of *Billboard*, would always go anywhere at once. It was ready to perform whenever and wherever the opportunity presented itself. We did plays in theaters, churches, school auditoriums, private homes. Barnstormed, too. There were frequent trips to towns in the vicinity of Savannah: Guyton, Millen, Clio, Statesboro. Macon made an offer but it was too far away. Most of our plays we did were of my own composition. We got others from the Samuel French Company and we also presented condensed versions, our own haphazard and unauthorized versions, of some of the road successes that trouped through Georgia. "Paid in Full," for one. "St. Elmo," for another. And "The Wolf" and "The Count of Monte Cristo." Catholic institutions were the Minor Stock Company's sponsors on several occasions and presentations under such auspices were invariably successful, for their officers and members were zealous in their support and in their ticket-selling. The Minor Stock Company reached its peak, and the close of its career, with the pro-

duction of a comedy called "His Own Home Town" at
the Savannah Theater, that historic institution fronting on
Bull Street and Chippewa Square. It was a Catholic char-
ities benefit and an absolute sell-out, the biggest crowd the
Savannah had had since William Hodge played "The Man
From Home." The author and leading player of "His
Own Home Town" was W. M. The script was later sent,
at the insistence of Henrietta Browne, a well-known stock
actress, to John Craig at the Castle Square Theater, Boston. Craig and Mary Young were forever in quest of new
talent; they were experimentalists in a day when nearly
every city had its resident stock company, when all of
America was a training school for Broadway. John Craig
eventually returned the play. He wrote a long and interesting letter. Liked the idea. The dialogue was pretty good.
But, he asked, where's your second act? This was a query
that I was to have difficulty answering in later years.

I wrote fiction under the formidable nom de plume of
J. Alexander Finn for the *Blue and White*, monthly publication of the Savannah High School. Later the Atlanta
newspapers printed and paid for sports correspondence
from the college town of Dahlonega, up in the red-clay
hills near the northern rim of the state. I felt that I was
being drawn to newspaper work but I wanted to hold off
as long as possible. Hold off and hold out for the theater. I
was pretty vague as to just how I was going to get into it,

but if questioned as to my talents and experience I could cite my Savannah stock company and my experience as Memorial Day orator at Dahlonega. I'd gone on in the football scene with a touring company of "The College Widow" (the Ty Cobb company), had played a few bits with the E. A. Schiller Players and had appeared as Dick the Rat in Henrietta Browne's presentation of "Alias Jimmy Valentine," unlocking a lock with a hairpin in the first act scene in the warden's office, Sing Sing prison. Miss Browne had told me to be sure and look her up when I came North. So said Mr. Schiller and Miss Irene Timmons and Alexander Leftwich. But I wasn't North and saw slim chance of getting there. Bull Street had its own drama legends. And it was wide and full of great shade trees and monuments to Revolutionary heroes. But it wasn't Broadway.

My eighteenth birthday was past. The North Georgia Agricultural College wasn't a gateway to writing or to acting. Should I go back to Miss Julia Boyle and tell her I wanted to take up art seriously? Should I take the place that my father was offering me in his big manufacturing plant out on the Augusta Road, and with the chance of some day being a member of the firm? Or should I march down to the office of the afternoon paper, the *Savannah Press*, and tell Pleasant A. Stovall, who was to be appointed Minister to Switzerland, and W. G. Sutlive, a dynamo of a

managing editor, that I wanted to go to work. . . . Or
what? . . . It was in such a moment of tormenting in-
decision that a stranger came to town. His hair was long
and thick and black and it hung shaggily about his ears
and neck. He had a large nose, cold clear eyes and the
booming voice of a tragedian. His years were numberless.
His name was Richmond. He was an itinerant Shakespearean reader.

I heard Richmond's Savannah reading and was impressed. The next morning I called on him at his hotel.
He was a man of abundant unction. He was trouping the
South, a one-man show. He knew all the rôles and all the
tricks: Lear, Hamlet, Iago. He liked Antony's speech to
the Romans and now and then he'd stray into the senti-
mentalities of "East Lynne" or into the absurdities of an
old farce, such as "Slasher and Crasher." Yes, he said, he
could use a spry young assistant. He had big things ahead.
For one thing, a week in Washington. For another a tour
of clean, green New England. Perhaps in Washington he'd
pay the President a call. He'd known several Presidents.
No—and he was quite firm about this—he wasn't one to
encourage anybody to a stage career. It was a hard life.
But if I really thought I was up to it, and thought I could
prove a quick study in passages from "Macbeth" and
"Cyrano de Bergerac," I might join him in Asheville. He'd
wire me. Two weeks later he did—collect. My father didn't

like that. He suggested that I drop the whole idea. But I went to Asheville.

Our town-to-town adventures went like this:

Johnson City, Tenn. didn't care for Shakespeare, or even snatches from "The Cricket on the Hearth." Bristol, that geographically indecisive town—one-half is in Virginia and the other half is in Tennessee—gave us a chance. C. R. arranged a reading before a business college and I remember to this instant the pained look on the face of the college president at the conclusion. In Abingdon, Va., where you now see Paula Tanqueray in exchange for a sack of oats at the box office of the Barter Theater, we were a forlorn duo and C. R. cursed me roundly for going up in my few scant lines. I think the bill was a combination of "Hamlet" and "Fritz in Ireland." In Pulaski, Va. my friend made an enormous hit in a diversified program, appearing in the parlor of a private home. It rained that night, however, and our takings were around $7. In Wytheville, Va. we borrowed $2 from a Methodist minister he had encountered in his wanderings. And in Roanoke, which was on down the line, we had our final little talk as we sat on a park bench at dusk. Our combination, he'd decided, hadn't worked out. The money I'd contributed to the tour was already used up on expenses. He'd decided, too, that it would be best for both if we'd go our separate ways. He said he had just enough fare to get him to Lynchburg. He gave me $1, a tattered copy of "Richard II," and some sage advice: "What you must do, my son, is to learn to rustle for yourself." And he was off. I rustled for a week. I picked cherries, slept in the park and the Y. M. C. A., and finally got a place at $35 a month in the employ of the Norfolk & Western Railway, a circumstance from which that carrier has never fully recovered. Only last summer I revisited Roanoke. The clocks spun back. The city seemed unchanged. As I walked its streets and wandered through its parks I had the feeling that at almost any minute I'd run across a quaint fellow with shaggy hair and a great deep voice strolling aimlessly and intoning passages from "Nell Gwynne" and Antony's Address to the Romans.

I held that Norfolk & Western job through a broiling summer, became friends with an undertaker—I had a $5-a-month room just above his parlors—and wrote a play. By the time I reached the third act I had written the undertaker into it. He was a fellow with an owlish look, a jumpy manner and given to fits of brooding, as well as to long periods of unexplained gaiety. He'd done a bit of drama study himself and often suggested that I give him a take-off on Petruchio or Sir Charles Surface or that rascally Bob Acres, but it was not until the summer was about gone that I agreed. It was a rainy evening in late August. Mortuary trade wasn't brisk and there, in the sombre snugness of his parlors, I read—and thought I read rather well—passages from "The Two Orphans." The gloom which had possessed him for days suddenly vanished. He became seized with terrific merriment, put on his hat and coat, and saying that he was going down to the Elks for some billiards and a beer dashed out the door. I never saw him again.

Nor did I ever see the railroad office again. I just left, and am sure that it was all right with the N. & W. I had my ample summer's savings and I went to Washington and to Poli's theater, which belonged to the famous stock circuit of the time. I laid my completed manuscript—this one was "The Man Who Owns the Blue Ridge"—upon the desk of a man named Thatcher. He was pleasant but not encouraging. No, Poli's didn't go in for new scripts, no matter how good they might be. No, they didn't ever hire any actors except people they got from Broadway. He suggested that I try New York on both counts. I had great yearning to go on North. But the South seemed so sure and so comfortable. I'd been away for more than three months. I put my manuscript in my bag and began my retreat from the Potomac.

So the theater, for the time being, was out. The Atlantic Coast Line bore me back South and I went direct to the *Press* office from the Union Station. Bill Flythe, the city editor, took me in to see W. G. Sutlive. Sutlive, human, undersized, likeable, looked up from his typewriter and laughed.

"Hell," he said, "What's the matter with the road? I thought you were an actor."

I said that perhaps I wasn't after all.

Well, he said, he'd seen me in a couple of those Savannah shows and he was inclined to agree with me.

We both laughed. His was heartier than mine.

But my newspaper career began then and there. I was to work without pay for a few months. I began doing general assignments, little stuff, took over the hotels as a regular run and also started a daily column for the sports page. For a byline I revived an old alias, J. Alexander Finn.

In my later prowlings of Broadway I encountered many players who came into the South, generally discovering that the years have done cruel things to the stalwarts and the beauties of the erstwhile road shows, but I never set eyes again upon my friend the Shakespearean reader. I did meet a man on the tiny Eltinge elevator who looked fearfully like him but it wasn't Mr. R.; just a bit actor who'd been out with Walter Hampden and who was poking about the Woods office trying to get into the cast of "The Shanghai Gesture."

In those immediate pre-Crash years, certainly prosperous ones for the drama, the new-trend playwrights, those who had developed so remarkably since "Beyond the Horizon" marked the ending of one era and the beginning of a new, were asserting themselves. They were writing hits. O'Neill gave the stage his nine acts of "Strange Interlude" and the town reveled in it. (Woollcott, disliking it, was a tart dissenter; Gabriel, loving it, wrote one of the best reviews of his life.) Robert E. Sherwood came along with "The Road to Rome." Sidney Howard, after some failings, contributed "They Knew What They Wanted" and "The Silver Cord." Elmer Rice re-established himself with "Street Scene." Philip Barry, not yet given to the metaphysical, was represented by a glossy comedy, "Paris Bound" and the almost equally engaging "Holiday." Maurine Watkins, who brought further proof that a woman can turn out a vivid play now and then, wrote "Chicago." John Van Druten, young London dramatist, gave Broadway "Young Woodley," which George C. Tyler produced without the change of more than a line or two, as Belasco had done with Eugene Walter's "The Easiest Way." George S. Kaufman and Edna Ferber, now working as a team, offered "Minick," to be followed by such pieces as "The Royal Family," "Dinner At Eight" and "Stage Door." Dramatists from out of the city room, Ben Hecht, Charlie MacArthur and Bartlett Cormack, proved themselves craftsmen of vitality. Hecht & MacArthur did that vigorous comic strip of newspaper life, "The Front Page" and Cormack gave Broadway "The Racket," in which there were memorable performances by Edward G. Robinson and John Cromwell. But of all

the plays from 1926 to and through 1929 there were two
that seemed, to my notion, to stand out in a class by themselves. They were vastly different in content. One was
"Journey's End," the war play so beautifully written by
R. C. Sherriff of England and the other was the melodramatic masterpiece, "Broadway," which affected the careers
of a dozen persons.

"Broadway" belongs to the legends; certainly to the
plays-I-wish-I-could-see-again lists of probably all those
beholding it during its long run at the Broadhurst. A fame-
maker, that melodrama, if there ever was one. It brought
riches to nearly all who touched it: Jed Harris, George
Abbott, Phil Dunning, and to Vinton Freedley and Alex
Aarons, lessees of the Broadhurst, where it was performed.
The dark, dour, emaciated, brooding and brilliant Jed
Harris began his spectacular producing spurt with this taut
and entertaining melodrama of romance and murder in
the Paradise Night Club. George Abbott became the
director-wizard of the theater of the moment. Lee Tracy,
who'd done only minor rôles, gave a crackling performance as the hoofer and was on his way. Tracy had been
waiting his chance. I first encountered him during rehearsals of "The Book of Charm," a small-town comedy
by John Kirkpatrick, which Rachel Crothers was directing. Tom Weatherly was the press agent and he'd been
told that I'd always wanted to play Hamlet but would

settle for a grave digger or less. He suggested that I do the
brief rôle of the book salesman, a gabby fellow who
bobbed up for just a minute, spoke his piece and vanished.
Miss Crothers was pleasant enough about it but quite dubious. She gave me a reading. Two. Three. Then she suggested that I step aside and let Lee Tracy read. Well, here
was the professional vs. Savannah stock. Tracy was breezy
and believable, just as he was in the rôle of the brother-
inventor in George Kelly's fine comedy, "The Show-Off."
He got that part only because of the unforgettable laugh,
the uncontrolled and scene-shaking guffaw, of the late
Louis John Bartels. George Kelly and Rosalie Stewart had
wanted Walter Catlett for the rôle but Ziegfeld asked
$1,500 weekly for Catlett. The play went into rehearsal
shy an actor for the most important character, Aubrey
Piper, the magnificent braggart, who clerked for the Pennsylvania Railroad. Bartels was in the brother part. One day
Kelly or Rosalie just happened to hear him laugh. He was
asked to laugh again, just that way. Rehearsal stopped.
Here was the man for Aubrey Piper. He rehearsed the
part, played it, and was such a success that his $150 weekly
salary was increased to $500 immediately after the Broad-
way opening. Tragic about Bartels. He was a one-play
triumph. He'd waited a long time for a hit. He never got
another. He died in Hollywood in 1932, his "Show Off"
glory dimmed.

"Broadway," as I've intimated, brought good fortune to numerous persons, myself included. Numerous others were associated with its early history but did not stick with it. I have in mind Miriam Hopkins and William A. Brady. She was offered, and she rejected, the rôle of the heroine when the play, then under the sole authorship of Phil Dunning, bore the title of "Bright Lights." Brady was interested and could have had the piece but, realizing its need for rewriting, let it get away. It was later that Jed Harris, Crosby Gaige and George Abbott came into the picture. I met Miriam Hopkins in 1924 in the office of Lyman Brown, one flight up in West Forty-fifth Street. She was in a show with music, then playing a try-out engagement in Stamford. She was having a dreadful time, wanted to get out, and it was up to the Chamberlain Brown office, then one of the busiest agencies, to tear up her contract. Clad in a full-length squirrel coat, she fairly hurtled herself into the office and it was my instant impression that here was one of the most attractive human beings I had ever seen. It was an opinion shared at the time, if not in later years, by Richard Watts, Jr., then the cane-carrying assistant movie reviewer ($30 weekly) who was making the Broadway rounds with me on that winter afternoon. She talked breathlessly and entertainingly; her charm and personality were fairly overpowering. Lyman Brown, who had placed her in that Stamford musical piece, was helpless. Certainly she had a contract. Certainly she was obligated to stay with the play, but certainly he would get her out of it. And so he did.

When "Broadway" was eventually produced at the Broadhurst the name of George Abbott appeared on the house-boards as co-author as well as director. The first night was terrific. When the curtain fell on Act One the play was a smash. When the last curtain fell people cheered. When William A. Brady read the notices the next morning he lit a cigar and said he guessed he had passed up a million dollars. That's the way with show business. Brady had a similar experience in Chicago when he got cold on "Within the Law" and sold out to the brothers Selwyn for a meager $10,000.

There was acclaim for nearly everybody now associated with "Broadway." Honors for Jed Harris, for Abbott, for Phil Dunning. For the players: Lee Tracy, Paul Porcasi, Sylvia Field, Billy Foran, John Wray, Tommy Jackson. There was really something of a tumult over the quiet, forceful, underplaying of Jackson in the rôle of Dan Mc-Corn, the hardboiled detective who had a heart. If Tommy Jackson had not appeared in "Broadway" and had not made such a hit, I would probably not have experienced such ease in getting "Gentlemen of the Press" on a New York stage.

I began the actual writing of "Gentlemen of the Press"

in 1927. The principal character, Wick Snell, veteran newspaperman, who'd been everywhere and seen everything, was inspired by a man who sat next to me on the rewrite desk at the *Tribune*—Arthur James Pegler, father of Westbrook Pegler. He fumed and he snarled about the injustices of newspaper life; he'd been in the business too long, he'd say, and he'd gotten too little out of it. He was hard and bitter and rasping but, underneath, there was a soft, kindly side, all of which went into the writing of the character of Snell. When I was done with the first act I went to the Lambs Club to see Edward Ellis, now of Hollywood. He was the perfect actor for my leading character. Ellis was polite, somewhat interested, but not particularly encouraging. I later met Leonard Gallagher in Sardi's and outlined the play to him. He was then associated with Guthrie McClintic, who was serving as producer-director for the Actors' Theater and who had brought forth a bright hit in "Saturday's Children," the comedy by the rising Maxwell Anderson. McClintic and Gallagher took an option on the play and told me to go ahead. But before I was midway in the second act the writing of "Gentlemen of the Press" had become one of the major industries of New York. I had collected four collaborators. When all else concerning the play is forgotten the story of the Five Authors will live on. It was almost fatal showmanship, the whole idea. It was five chins thrust out, not just one. But the legend persists and I shall try accurately to set down the credits. My co-writers were my close friends and they were all co-frequenters of the Chez Florence, Texas Guinan's and the Hotsy Totsy. I hereby present the quartet, alphabetically: Mark Barron of Waco, Texas, John S. Cohen, Jr., of Atlanta, Willard Keefe of Morton, Minn., and Richard Watts, Jr. of Charleston, W. Va. Barron wrote a little dialogue and was a consultant on numerous scenes. Cohen didn't do any writing but delivered himself of some grave and abstract counsel and insisted on putting sex into the second act. Keefe assisted in the writing of several scenes, suggested the curtain of the first act, wrote the best laugh line of the show, and contributed to the general excitement, and to the distress of George Abbott, by falling backstage on the final night at the Apollo, Atlantic City, and suffering a broken leg. Watts didn't do any writing but he was ever-present and was fiercely loyal to the project before and after production.

The title of "Gentlemen of the Press"—an excellent one, I always thought—was contributed by Elbert Severance, who was with the brothers Chanin, architects and theater-builders. The play was finished in December of 1927 and on Christmas Eve the Rialto Typing Service delivered the scripts—original and five carbons. The prettiest script, the one with the red-ribbon trimmings, went to McClintic and

Gallagher. Another to Miriam Hopkins and another to
Eloise Taylor, now Mrs. Pat O'Brien of Hollywood, who
had joined the Five Authors in their nightly rovings and
who had heard so much of the dialogue she knew the play
line for line. Heard so much that she'd been talking to
Tommy Jackson about it, for she had now joined the
"Broadway" company as one of the girls of the Paradise
Cabaret. Tommy had long had yearnings to produce a
play; such inclinations were pretty general in those prosperous pre-Crash years. Now he'd made a hit, he was paid
every week, and getting good money. All he wanted was a
script. He read "Gentlemen of the Press" behind scenes at
the Broadhurst and the next morning he got me on the
phone at *The Sun*. Tommy was tough and plain-talking.
He said: "I like that goddam show. I'll buy it and produce
it. Find out what McClintic is going to do about it." Several days later McClintic, en route to Seattle, sent a wire
releasing the manuscript. At 11 A.M. on New Year's Eve,
in his office near the Algonquin, Tommy signed the contract for the rights to "Gentlemen of the Press" and paid
$500. We began talking about actors. About directors.
About try-out towns. It all seemed so swift. And so easy.
I went to the New Year's Eve party of the Mayfair Club
with the feeling that the play would be in rehearsal within
a month.

But it was not quite that easy. Bankroll trouble developed. Tommy Jackson and Hy Kraft, who had become associated with him, peddled the script for backing. Two months passed. I was pretty dejected about the whole business and, after heavy conference with the authorship board—Keefe, Barron, Watts and Cohen—began planning to resell the play after the option expired. Finally, however, Jackson sent the script to George Abbott. Lightning struck. Abbott liked it and said he'd direct it. He suggested a late summer opening instead of a spring production. His name meant then, as it does now, money at the box office, and Jackson & Kraft got a backer within an hour. They could have had a dozen. John Cromwell, who had been playing in "The Racket," was engaged for the rôle of Snell. Abbott was precise in his casting; he can pass on more players in a given time than any director I've ever known. He had many suggestions for script revision and most of them were good ones. At the beginning of the summer I went to Colorado for a brief stay, wrote an entirely new third act, returned to Broadway and lost it in a taxi! It had to be done over again, and immediately.

We went into rehearsal late in July and hoped to get to town ahead of the competitive newspaper piece, "The Front Page," written by Ben Hecht and Charles MacArthur and produced by Jed Harris. Jed, however, brought in his play in mid-August. "Gentlemen of the Press" played a week in Atlantic City prior to New York

and during that week the Five Authors must have turned
George Abbott's hair white. Nobody, certainly none of
the five (put up at the Hotel Shelburne at the expense of
the management) was ever late for rehearsal, no training
rules were broken, but Abbott always feared the worst.
Abbott is a man who doesn't drink or smoke and he mildly
disapproves of those who do either or both. He has, however, his social side and he is something of a tea-room Don
Juan. There never was a man who cared more for dancing, and when he invites a lady out for an evening of dancing she dances! He managed to get in a few waltzes at
Atlantic City after putting his authors safely to bed. After
a week at the shore—the theater was the famous old Apollo
—and with only minor catastrophe, "Gentlemen of the
Press" moved on to Broadway and opened at Henry Miller's, on what must have been the hottest night of the
year. It was a big opening; a complete sell-out. The orchestra floor could have been sold five times. I stayed away
from Forty-third Street, getting the returns at a speakeasy
known as the Aquarium. Dorothy Hall and Neal Andrews
gave a tremendous after-theater party in Fifty-seventh
Street. I got about 400 telegrams. I thought that was tremendous, only to learn that Gene Buck once received
2,000!

Some of the reviews were pretty severe, although several critics acknowledged the authenticity of the city-room

flavor. The Five Authors build-up had its bearing upon the notices. Gilbert Gabriel, writing in *The Sun*, began his comment with the following sentence: "This is where a critic needs a friend and loses five." Heywood Broun, reviewing for the *Telegram*, paid tribute to the true atmosphere, the characters and the dialogue, but said the story wasn't as strong as that of "The Front Page." The Five Authors were about ready to head for the East River in a body when things began happening. Paramount called and asked for a price on the film rights. There was inquiry about the London rights (which we sold). A. L. Jones, then of the firm of Jones & Green, and operating the Forty-eighth Street Theater, talked of moving the play into his house. And then *Variety* came out. Jack Lait wrote a beautiful notice, saying that "Gentlemen of the Press" explored the very hearts and souls of newspapermen. And on Saturday evening of the opening week we had a big sale.

Paramount closed a deal within three weeks. Al Jones took over the management and "Gentlemen of the Press" stayed in Forty-eighth Street until nearly Christmas and went on tour in January. During the fall of '28 several of the critics, Gabriel and Broun included, returned for second glimpses of the play. They both wrote new pieces, glowing pieces. Had we received these notices in August instead of November the play might have taken ranking as an actual hit.

There was a character in the piece called Bellflower, the
name of an Atlanta newspaperman and a name that had
always fascinated me. The Atlanta Bellflower was a police
reporter, the leg-man type who made friends with the cops
and the lawyers and the bail bondsmen and who got a lot
of news. I didn't put Bellflower as a person into the play;
just his name. The actor who created the rôle of Bellflower—one of the skimpiest ever written into the American drama—was that renowned trouper, Russel Crouse.
He belonged to New York's writing set, was married to
Alison Smith (who did some excellent reviews for the
*Morning World*) and he conducted a column on the editorial page of the *Evening Post*. He got a lot of copy out
of his stage experience but along about Thanksgiving he
decided that he had had enough. Here, at last, was my
chance. A chance to act and one that wouldn't lead, neces-
sarily, to a park bench in Roanoke. Saul Abraham, one of
the best-known of the Broadway treasurers and a fellow
who had great popularity among the Broadway news-
getters, was general manager for Jones. William Fields, a
Texan come to New York and a leader in his craft, was
press agent. The three of us talked Jones into letting me
go on as Crouse's replacement. Crouse got $60 weekly. Or
could it have been $75? But Al Jones, who had always pro-
tested that actors and authors were overpaid, shaved me to
$50. Well, I got an Equity card and played Bellflower in

Manhattan and Brooklyn. When the show was ready to move on to Baltimore I left the cast. Jones was cutting expenses. So the character was just dropped from the play.

I bought a car, clothes, a motorboat (which I never used), paid my bills, put away some money for travel and leased an apartment, a walk-up, and midway in the fascinating Fifty-eighth Street block between Fifth and Madison avenues. I'd now known Jeanne Eagels since "Rain" and had been frequently to her country houses. We met one afternoon at Le Mirliton, that charming and delightful little restaurant in Fifty-eighth Street which George Kuhnert has been running for all these years. I told her about my new place upstairs. She wanted to see it immediately. It was exactly what she wanted, she decided. A midtown walk-up, just a tiny place where she could stay when she didn't feel like driving to Westchester. I introduced her to Mrs. Packard, the landlady. Two days later Jeanne Eagels moved into her two-room walk-up above the fruit shop. She wanted to read and sleep and rest. But to her modest quarters she brought cook, maid and chauffeur and I believe there were times when even a butler put in an appearance. Before the coming of the erstwhile Sadie Thompson, life above the fruit shop had never been particularly serene but now, once she had moved in, there was forever bustle on the stairway. Friends began dropping in. The two-room hideaway became something of a salon.

There came an afternoon when the crush was so great that
she left her callers to their gaieties and fled to her Westchester house for peace, only to find that it, too, was over-
run with guests. A great actress, Jeanne Eagels, I thought.
And how singular it was (and what a loss for the theater!)
that she and Emily Stevens and Holbrook Blinn should all
die within a short time of each other. Miss Stevens and
Blinn died in 1928. The following year saw the passing of
Jeanne Eagels. Her death came with shocking sudden-
ness. She had called at the Park Avenue Hospital in the
late afternoon of October 3, 1929 and was waiting a con-
sultation with her personal physician when a convulsion
seized her. Death was attributed by the city toxicologist
to an overdose of chloral hydrate. The body, in a silver
and bronze coffin, was sent for burial to her native Kansas
City, which she left in her teens to make her fame in New
York.

Jeanne Eagels had moved from Fifty-eighth Street but
I continued seeing her frequently. I was not at *The Sun*
office when news of her death was received. But when I
reached my typewriter the next morning there was a typed
memo rolled into the machine. It read: "Please call Jeanne
Eagels, 3:10 P.M."

Richard Lockridge was now dramatic critic of *The Sun*,
having been given the job in November of 1928 when
Gilbert Gabriel went to the *American*. Lockridge, born

in St. Joseph, Mo., was with the Kansas City *Star* immediately prior to his coming to *The Sun*. In Keats Speed's years as an executive—he has been a New York managing editor continuously since 1907, except for the two years that he was running the Atlanta *Georgian*—he has always had the feeling that men who have worked in Atlanta and Kansas City have had pretty thorough training. And Lockridge, arriving in 1923, was readily hired. He proved himself expert at rewrite and also did second-string reviews. So when Gabriel, against his own better judgment, capitulated to Hearst's offer and became, as the *American's* critic, one of the highest paid members of the craft, Lockridge moved into the spot that had been held in other years by Woollcott, Stephen Rathbun and Samuel Hoffenstein. Few of the first-line critics of the New York dailies over the past quarter of a century have been fired. It happened to Hoffenstein, however, and because of a review he wrote of a play by Edward Knoblauch called "Marie-Odile." This piece was produced by David Belasco at the Belasco Theater January 26, 1915. Hoffenstein's account of the play appeared in the *Evening Sun* of the following day. Harsh as it was, such a notice would scarcely bring about a critic's removal nowadays. But there was the legend, and it's another that persists, that Belasco made an appearance at the *Sun* office on the afternoon of January 27 to offer angry protest. I present, in part, Hoffenstein's comment:

" 'Marie-Odile' is anything you please but a play. Its form is narrative, and, written in a humorous vein, with considerable excision might make a tolerable story for a railroad journey. Call it, perhaps, a psychological study as unsuited to the stage as the mental processes of a child who has just been given its first dish of ice cream. Its central figure is a character absolutely without subjective life, and monstrous though it may seem, a character that does not appear to possess the capacity for development. After having passed through a most momentous experience in a woman's life we find her mentally and spiritually precisely where she began. . . . The play is lacking in struggle, in conviction, in suspense, in cumulative force, in human appeal, in every essential of dramatic writing.

"The play was staged with the producer's customary attention to detail. But of Miss Starr's performance of Marie-Odile it is unfair to say anything. Her business consisted in being naïve and innocent and saccharine, and all that she was to perfection. She talked sweetly, walked with fascinating resilience and looked charming. But there are at least twenty-five thousand ladies in New York without predilections for the stage

who, with proper training—especially in the art
of being unsophisticated—could have done the
same thing. To say of an actress of Miss Starr's
standing that she accomplished these things is like
praising her art by saying that she is good to her
mother."

And such was the prose that cost a critic his job in the
New York of nearly a quarter of a century ago. Hoffenstein was immediately hired as press agent for A. H.
Woods. Woods remembered a review Hoffy had done on
a piece called "He Comes Up Smiling," a play starring
Douglas Fairbanks. The notice had fascinated the producer. He sent for Hoffenstein and asked what the *Evening Sun* was paying him. "Sixty dollars a week," said the
ex-critic. "I won't pay you that," said Woods, spraying
his cigar ashes over his shirt front. "But I will pay you
$100 a week." It was a deal.

In January of 1929, with talking pictures experiencing
their nervous beginnings, with Hollywood still jittery over
the sudden collapse of the silent screen, and with an entire
country being wired for sound, Paramount began shooting
"Gentlemen of the Press" at its Astoria studio. Of course,
I'm one who has never quite understood why movies
are not always being made within the area of New York

City, which seems to have all the requirements except a few oranges, the Club Trocadero and Palm Springs for week-ends. But such is a problem, I suppose, that belongs to the Warners and the Schencks and the Zanucks.

Walter Huston was spotted by Jesse Lasky in George M. Cohan's (and Ring Lardner's) baseball play, "Elmer the Great," and given his first screen job—the rôle of Wick Snell. Huston had done everything else—the legitimate and vaudeville, rep, tent and tab, but here was a new and curious medium that excited and delighted him. Charles Ruggles was engaged for the comic, Betty Lawford for the ingénue-heroine, and the red-thatched Lawrence Leslie, a brilliant young actor who died just as his career was beginning, played one of the newspaper boys. Monta Bell was the producer (he later married Betty Lawford); the late Millard Webb was the director; John Meehan, now of Hollywood, was supervisor of dialogue and I was hired to put in some spare time on supervision of city room atmosphere. Bartlett Cormack had done the screen play. With the shooting ready to start it was discovered that there was no actress for the rôle of Myra, siren of the piece. So we all went immediately to Tony's and there, in the haze of that famous back room, with Forney Wyly, the Atlanta wit, making cracks at everybody in sight, and with celebrities of sorts piling over the bare tables, we found Kay Francis. She was resting comfortably behind a Tom

Collins. She was tall, dark and interesting-looking but had made far more appearances in Tony's than she had on the Broadway stage. She looked the part of Myra, all right. But the day of just looking it was gone forever. Could she act and how was her voice? She was hustled over to Astoria. In the first test her voice came through strong and clear and vibrant. Her screen career began that very day.

Early in March of 1929 I went abroad—my first trip. I sailed on the *S.S. Columbus* with Jack Yorke, Mark Barron and the Theater Guild's "Porgy" troupe, a brilliant ensemble. Frank Wilson, Rose McLendon, Jack Carter, Percy Verwayne, Richard Huey, Leigh Whipper, Georgette Harvey, Wesley Hill—the finest talent that the negro stage afforded. The fable of Charleston's Catfish Row, which had been such a rousing success in New York, was warmly received by the London press but not the public. It wasn't a successful engagement and the Harlem negroes were glad when the end came. Most of them had a miserable time in London. They were homesick. And London was dark. And it was foggy. And it was cold. They were not welcome at the good hotels and they scattered through the city, putting up in rooming houses. The English money confused them and so did the English people. Most of them got to London broke, had to begin drawing advances, and kept it up during the entire stay. A few of the dandies of the troupe went in lavishly for the fine English clothes and it was only two or three days after arrival, when strolling Bond Street, a familiar face came toward me. The face I knew, but not the raiment. It was one of the "Porgy" actors, now wearing spats and monocle, striped trousers, carrying a cane and topping it off with a beret. He was magnificent.

Mark Barron and I went first to the Hotel Piccadilly and then to the Mayfair. We'd hardly entered the Mayfair quarters when the operator announced, "Paris calling." It was the warm, friendly, crackling voice of A. H. Woods. "Sweetheart," he said, "get the hell on over here. Paris is wonderful. I think I'll move my office here. Come on over and meet me at the Scribe." That was the Al Woods of 1929, the hearty, vigorous, exuberant, reckless, take-a-chance, go-anywhere-at-once showman from New York's Forty-second Street—the producer of a hundred hits, the man who hired Mary Pickford at $75 a week in "The Fatal Wedding," who gave Ronald Colman his start, who made a million with "The Trial of Mary Dugan," and who had had five—or was it six?—successes running in New York simultaneously. Al Woods, of the pre-Crash era, who kept his money in cash in a safety deposit box. He once showed me a key and said that it would unlock a box that contained one thousand thousand dollar bills. He contributed color to the New York stage through many sea-

sons and Broadway news coverage was always more interesting when he was active. His present rôle is that of
something of a non-combatant, but he has never been a
bitter man nor one easily discouraged. He continues his
search for that elusive hit and will tell you that his biggest
success is yet ahead of him. "I'll get one, sucker," he'll say.
"Look at Bill Brady. He was in a tough spot when 'Street
Scene' came along. Sure, I'll get one. It's just the breaks,
ain't it? An office boy can write a million dollar hit these
days. And the funny part of it is, most of 'em are tryin'."

I immediately began my London playgoing and copy-
writing, sending back "London After Dark" pieces via the
fast boats. The London plays weren't very good (are they
ever?) but the people of the West End theater were
gracious and friendly and I regretted leaving at the end of
ten days. I was trying, however, to keep to a certain
schedule and cover a lot of ground in a limited time. I took
the cross-channel plane to Paris and went immediately to
the Hotel Scribe in quest of Al Woods. But just that day
he had decided to return to America. He was probably
getting aboard the boat train at that very minute.

A week in Paris, continuing my copy-writing and making contacts for visits that were to come. One of my objec-
tives on this 1929 trip was Greece, which I reached via the
airline and via Vienna, Budapest and Belgrade. I had several delightful days at the seaport of Salonika and went high

into the Balkans astride a burro. And there, on a mountain top, dined with a Greek who had formerly been in business at Coney Island. He had a stand in Stillwell Avenue, around the corner from Steeplechase. Made money, too. And he'd come home to stay.

In Athens, the evening before flying to Naples, via Corfu, I stood on the terrace of the Hotel Grande Bretagne. A plane, zooming perilously low over Constitution Square, broke the stillness of the Athenian twilight. I was contemplating the distant Acropolis, beautiful in the fading daylight, and began talking with a small, slight, dark man who stood near by.

"New York," he said, suddenly and quietly, "is a town I like. I like it because it's such a clean-looking city and because you see so many pretty girls as you stroll the streets. I'll be back there before long and I'm wondering what changes I'll find. . . ."

And into the Grande Bretagne's little bar I went with my new friend, Dikran Kouyoumdjian, who was born in Roustchouk, Bulgaria. To America, and to the book readers of the world, he is known as Michael Arlen.

## London to Cairo

"IF YOU WANT A GREAT STORY," JIM GORDON HAD SAID TO me, as he introduced me to the Greek beverage, ouzo, at a little water-front bar at Salonika, "go to Persia. Go to Teheran and interview the Shah. There's an amazing fellow. He once rode into Teheran on a pony and now he owns the place." Jim Gordon, one of the rare human beings of the world, and such as you seldom have the good fortune to encounter in your wanderings, had been to Teheran. He'd been all over. Istanbul, Bagdad, Bombay, Luxor. An American, who went abroad in the service of the American Express. And now, as we sipped our ouzo while gazing upon Mount Olympus, I assured him that I'd try to get to Persia.

But I never did. When I set out on another jaunt in the spring of 1930 I planned a series of "After Dark" columns that would take me from the Thames to the Caspian Sea, down across Persia, and westward again via Bagdad. But my easternmost point was Aleppo, Syria. For a time I considered giving up on the Near East entirely; for London on this trip was gayer and even friendlier than it had been

the year before. London was alive with good column copy.
And when I got to France, particularly when I reached
Saint-Antoine Du Rocher (Indre-et-Loire) it was my
inclination to stay on for years and years.

I went to London's Savoy this time, one of the great
hotels of this planet, and always throbbing with cos-
mopolite activity. The Savoy in London, Twenty-one in
New York and the George V in Paris and you see the
same faces. They're generally interesting faces. The
Savoy's grill was thronged nightly, and, as always, by the
people of the London theater and by members of the
Broadway-in-Piccadilly colony. . . . C. B. Cochran, Ray-
mond Massey, lovely Benita Hume, Richard Bird, Joyce
Barbour, John Van Druten, Gladys and Leslie Henson,
Isabel Jeans, Marc Connelly, Guy Bolton, Gilbert Miller,
Peggy Wood, and Claire Luce, who seems to have a gayer
time in sheer living than anyone else I can think of. I was
sending back London copy, a piece for every day, and
mailing it in batches of three and four articles at a time. I
frequented the Savoy and the Mayfair and the Carlton and
the Ivy. I strolled the Embankment and went to Lime-
house and took a trip up the Thames and many rides into
the country, including a delightful week-end in Sevenoaks,
but there was never time, for one in quest of copy of people and copy of the theater, for the routine seeing of London. For me it's still a great giant of a city, fascinating in

the utmost, but unexplored save for portions in the vicinity
of the Strand. During this stay of 1930 I met Barrie, got a
pleasant note from Shaw, interviewed Pinero and A. A.
Milne, lunched several times with C. B. Cochran, saw the
shows with Vinton Freedley and had my first meeting
with Tallulah Bankhead, calling on her at No. 1 Farm
Street, just off Berkeley Square. She was then triumphant
in "La Dame aux Camelias."

The session with Pinero and the visit in Farm Street
were accomplished between 10 A.M. and 6 P.M. That eve-
ning Freedley and I went to Wyndham's to see Charles
Laughton in Edgar Wallace's gangster piece, "On the
Spot." We were thrilled by the playing of Laughton but
almost equally impressed by the underplaying of young
Emlyn Williams, who has been coming ahead ever since.
We joined Marc Connelly and Constance Carpenter and
some other London playmates for after-theater supper.
And from 1 A.M. until the Thames glimmered in the dawn
just out my window I pounded away at my portable. The
"London After Dark" copy had to make the next boat, the
*Berengaria.*

I found Sir Arthur Wing Pinero, at 115-A Harley
Street, living alone on the second floor of a two-story
house. He was then seventy-five, somewhat deaf and he
walked shakily. I'd seen him before at a distance—the distance of across the grill of the Savoy—and I'd been told of

his prawn-whisker eyebrows. Thick, bushy, unruly, fantastic. His great vitality seemed to be in his eyebrows. He was gracious but somewhat tremulous. Apparently he had few visitors and rarely received an interviewer. He lived there in comparative solitude, with the bookshelves of his study serving as attestation of his long, active and successful career as a dramatist. . . . "The Second Mrs. Tanqueray," "The Gay Lord Quex," "The Thunderbolt," "His House in Order," "Mid-Channel." Pinero, master of dramaturgy, lit his cigarette, sank into a heavy red leather chair and talked.

He said: "I am greatly indebted to the New York theater, far more so than I am to the theater of my native land. America has done more for me. The American playgoer has a quicker mind than the Englishman—quicker to grasp and appreciate a good play. New York has been wonderful to me. I have great affection for it. . . . America again? I hate to say it but it's been forty-five years since I was in your great country. I went over there to put on a comedy of mine, something called 'The Magistrate.' I stayed in a hotel around Union Square. I think it was called the Clarendon. . . . No, no, no. I could never go back to New York again. I'd be scared. I couldn't stand it." And he never did. In that very year death came to 115-A Harley Street, London, W.I.

Tallulah Bankhead represented Success in London. Little

American girl makes good in a foreign land. She was Success and she was also News. Her conquest of Broadway had failed but in London she was a hit, almost from the beginning. But wait. She'd show Broadway, and she'd say it a little grimly. There was never any lack of courage about Bankhead and she didn't then know there was anybody named Lillian Hellman and that there was to be a play called "The Little Foxes."

I reached Tallulah's house via one of those great, lumbering, cavernous, turn-on-a-dime taxis. Farm Street is a glorified alleyway, a crooked little street that goes along for a short distance, gets all confused and expires. Tallulah's house at No. 1 was squat, compact, two-storied. We had lunch. We talked. That is, she talked. She always talks. Swiftly, entertainingly, and about everything: Dumas and "Camille," "The Green Hat," Florentine sculpture, the Oxford-Cambridge boat race, the daffodil show, Jeanne Eagels (one of her great enthusiasms), Rachel Crothers, Cornell, matrimony. ("I want none of it," she cried, throatily.) And New York.

"New York?" . . . She sat on the floor, clothes up to her head, coiling herself about the pillows. "I want to play there again. I'd be curious and excited about it. But I live here, you see. I've been here seven years. I adore London. It's been nice to me. . . . I've made money but I haven't saved a penny. The taxes are terrible. . . . Why

am I doing 'Camille'? Well, they always say I'm doing
plays in which I undress. I've only undressed in two out
of fifteen—'Her Cardboard Lover' and 'The Garden of
Eden.' Just let them try to tell me I undress in 'La Dame
aux Camelias'! . . . In love? I should say not! If I ever do
fall in love I'll get married. . . . What else? Have another
cocktail. That's a good one John makes—brandy and gin.
. . . Glad you came in. I don't care what you say about
me but for Christ's sake make me out as having a sense of
humor!"

The page boy of the Hotel Savoy, all of four feet, bright
face and brighter buttons, was at my river-suite door. He
extended his tray. "Letter for you, sir. . . . Thank you
very much, sir."

I'd been expecting this letter. It was in ink and in writing that was fascinatingly minute:

Le Plessis
Saint-Antoine du Rocher
(Indre-et-Loire)

March 29th, 1930.

Dear Ward Morehouse:
Sure thing! I'll be glad to see you. Arrange to
come down and stay over night with us. There's
a good train from Paris to Tours around two or
two-thirty P.M. that gets in Tours around six.

Wire me a couple of days ahead so I'll be certain
to be here and say what day you're coming and
I'll meet you at Tours station. This place is ten
kilometers out in the country. You can get back
to Paris comfortably by the next evening if you're
in a hurry and still have a night and morning
here. I warn you I've got nothing much to offer
in the way of news since I don't want to declare
myself much in advance as to the nature of the
work I'm now doing. [It was "Mourning Becomes Electra."] I'm certain you'll like it here. I
can promise you a grand lungful of Touraine
country air and a spell of peaceful repose—and
you can give me the New York news!

All kindest regards,
EUGENE O'NEILL.

Eugene O'Neill, now in California, was then forty-one.
He and Mrs. O'Neill (Carlotta Monterey) had presumably happy years in the Touraine. They kept house, thirty-
five rooms of house, at Chateau Plessis, removed by a
hundred miles and more from the whir of Paris. Their
nearest neighbor, a French peasant, wasn't really near.
There, in the great gray chateau, isolated and austere,
near the river Loire and encircled by a beautiful wood,
he found the tranquillity which, seemingly, he had sought
and had never found in America.

I took the Golden Arrow out of London, my first
Channel crossing other than by plane, and was in Tours

the next afternoon. That evening, at Chateau Plessis, we sat before an open fire in the large, high-ceilinged living room. Eugene O'Neill talked freely until well past midnight of himself and his writings. His speech was always thoughtful; it was never hurried.

"If I had any idea," he said, "that I'd have to repeat myself, that I had to stand still, I'd quit writing plays. I'd call it a day. I write primarily for myself, because it is a pleasure, and it would cease to be that if I started repeating. I could have gone on forever with plays like 'Anna Christie,' or with the expressionism of 'The Hairy Ape,' but I'm interested in trying to do better things.

"Now, this new play of mine is the hardest thing I've ever tried. God knows, it's the most ambitious. I've done the first draft. I'll do a second, then lay that aside and start on something else. Later I'll come back to it, and perhaps I may have something. I don't want to talk of its content. That hurt me with 'Dynamo.' I just want to finish it, call a stenographer from Paris, and then mail it to the Guild. I've been at work on it for a year. Carlotta seems to think it's all right." ("Wonderful," was the word Mrs. O'Neill used to me.)

The dramatist-son of a grand old actor sipped his Coca-Cola and sat gazing at the burning wood chunks.

"You see," he said, "I've found out something. I've found out that I ought to take more time. Looking back to 'Dynamo,' I did eighteen long plays in eleven years. That's too much. If I could go back I'd destroy some of these plays, say, four of them—'Gold,' 'The First Man,' 'The Fountain,' and 'Welded.' I've written, I think, forty plays—twenty long and twenty short. In my notebook I have ideas for thirty plays, perhaps thirty-two. That's work for a lifetime."

"Would you," I asked, "destroy 'Dynamo'?"

"No, but I'd rewrite it. 'Dynamo' had in it the makings of a fine play, but I did it too fast. And it was silly of me to mention a trilogy. And I wasn't surprised that they jumped me about it—that was but natural after 'Strange Interlude.'"

He paused. "The play of mine," he said, "for which I have the greatest affection is 'The Great God Brown.' Next, 'The Hairy Ape' and then 'Strange Interlude.' My favorite short play is 'Moon of the Caribbees.' I think the best writing I've done for the theater was in 'Lazarus Laughed.'

"I've been remarkably lucky, I think, in the matter of actors. Certainly the performance of Walter Huston in 'Desire Under the Elms' was tremendous. Exactly what I had in mind. And there were splendid performances by Paul Robeson in 'The Emperor Jones' and by Lynn Fontanne in 'Strange Interlude.'"

We rode the next day in his Bugatti racer and got it

up to 106 kilometers an hour. We swam in his concrete pool and wandered over his forty acres, with his Gordon setter and Dalmatians coming along. Never one for chatter, Eugene O'Neill, but on this beautiful morning in the Touraine he talked rather constantly.

"I love it here," he said simply. "But I've never had any idea of living here permanently. No nonsense about renouncing America. There's such a thing as being sensibly patriotic. But living away from America has been a good way to get to know America—to see things you couldn't see before."

And so I found Eugene O'Neill when he lived in France. They told me good-bye as the chauffeur whirled through the driveway in Mrs. O'Neill's magnificent French car. He had on a heavy sweater and she was trim in smart Parisian sport clothes. He extended his hand and grinned. "Tell them we're coming back," he said. "We're coming to live in New York or Georgia or California or somewhere."

I was in the big car. The engine roared. The car shot forward and I was off for the Tours train, which was to take me back to the boulevards and the bewilderments of Paris.

I wanted to go to Cannes for an interview with Maxine Elliott but my several and importunate letters remained unanswered. The New York colony along the Riviera had dwindled, so I decided to push on East. In Milan, as the

Simplon Orient Express paused, I encountered Helen Gahagan. She was in Italy studying voice. She wanted to stay
in the theater but she also had hopes for grand opera. In
Sofia I attended what seemed a dreadful performance of
"The Trial of Mary Dugan" and the next day was presented to King Boris, the Bulgarian monarch who seemed
happiest when at the throttle of a locomotive. In Istanbul
I discovered, to my considerable consternation, that I had
arrived on the first day of a four-day national holiday
and the money sent on by *The Sun* could not be had
until the banks opened. I'd now decided to save the Shah
and Persia for another trip and was planning to get at
least as far as Bagdad. But members of the American colony in Istanbul protested. Why Bagdad? It wasn't worth
the time and expense. Go instead, they urged, to the Holy
Land and on to the Nile. Istanbul's holiday finally ended
and I set out for Jerusalem.

The Turkish express rattled across the brown and red
Asiatic plain. . . . The village of Sapanca, where a mob
of townsfolk besieged the train, yelping and pawing and
lifting baskets, filled with indescribable wares. . . . The
village of Ulukiska, and another howling village throng.
. . . High mountains, snowy peaks, and, after many hours,
across the frontier into Syria and the town of Aleppo, at
the extreme north of the vast Arabian peninsula and as
far from the Holy City of Mecca as Rome is from Lon-

don. . . . Camels in sight for the first time. Scores and scores of camels, hundreds of horses, thousands and thousands of sheep. . . . The Toros Express, shorn of several cars at Aleppo, took on new buoyancy and moved on to Ryak at a respectable speed. I just finished Edna Ferber's stirring "Cimarron" as Ryak was reached. And my thoughts were upon the great wild country that was Oklahoma, upon the oil fields and the oil-rich Indians and the rig-builders and the tool-dressers, upon the terror and tumult of the magnificent southwest, and upon Yancey Cravat, as I was borne, this time by motor, into the Holy Land.

Jerusalem broiled in the midday heat. I choked in the dust of Jaffa Road, went to Zion Hall for a few minutes of Al Jolson in "The Singing Fool," met a missionary who had once taught school in El Paso, got a drink at the New Era bar, a bath at the Grand New Hotel, glanced over the news in the *Palestine Bulletin*, talked with a thick-ankled girl from upstate New York who was taking a huddle of American tourists through the Garden of Gethsemane, inquired about the train schedules to Cairo (it was then a fifteen-hour ride) and went diligently about the business of seeing the town. . . . Christians, Moslems, Jews, Bedouins. Soldiers, monks, missionaries. Camels, sheep, goats, donkeys. Peddlers, water-sellers, beggars, money changers, white-robed traffic policemen. Wine and

spirits. American jazz shrieking from a phonograph shop.
The American Express. The Anglo-American Bar. Dust
and heat and flies. Jerusalem on a mid-May Sabbath.

I bargained with a taxi company and went to Jericho,
to the River Jordan and then to the Dead Sea, where I met
Mr. Saad. I shall never forget Theodore Saad. A Greek,
he spoke many languages, including excellent English. One
of the most interesting men you'd find in countless years
of travel. He operated a small restaurant at the northern
end of the Dead Sea, which stretches its salty length for
forty-six miles through the heart of Palestine. He had
visions of owning a big hotel and he thought the Dead
Sea could become one of the playgrounds of the world.
Capital would come for the exploitation of its shores.
Tourists would come for the benefits of its health-giving
water.

"I used to be an amateur chemist," said Mr. Saad, "and
I know. That water is no good for fish, but it's great for
humans. It has just everything in it—sodium bromide, sodium chloride, sulphur, bitumen, magnesium, potassium
iodide. . . . It's also great for swimming, because you
can't sink. You could go the whole length of it and no
harm could come to you."

Mr. Saad talked of many things. He'd been to New
York and Chicago and San Francisco. Perhaps it was San
Francisco he liked best. Arabia was a great vast country

that no one knew anything about. He feared there would always be terrorism in the Holy Land, that there could never be peace between the Arabs and the Jews. He feared for the future of the world and that whenever another war came, as it was sure to come, all the Near East would again be in it. He gave me a bed that night at the edge of the sea and the next morning I took a daybreak swim and breakfasted on Turkish coffee and eggs from Jerusalem, served by a giant black man who was born in Assuan, Egypt. At noon I was aboard a train, en route to the Suez.

Cairo: Shepheard's and Semiramis closed. Season gone and most of fashionable Egypt packed off to Switzerland and the Italian lakes. Dragomen idling about the Continental-Savoy, waiting for anything that looked like tourist prey. Italian opera at the Kursall, a Russian ballet at the Kit Kat. And a troupe of English players presenting "Journey's End." A handful of Europeans visiting the Sphinx and a lone Britisher resolutely ascending the big pyramid, which an Arab could do, to the top and back, in eight minutes—for a shilling. . . . Joseph Lancaster Brent, the young and engaging U. S. vice-consul, told me that the cotton crop and Egyptian independence were the topics of the country. . . . And in the Egyptian garden of the Continental-Savoy, beneath the date palms, a much-traveled matron asked about the news of Dallas and Fort Worth.

"You can't fool me, young man," she said. "I know a Texas accent when I hear it. I used to live in Amarillo. And in Florida, too. Now you sit right down here and tell me everything you've been doing and everywhere you've been and let me tell you about Luxor and the lower Nile." I sat. And I heard about Luxor and the lower Nile.

I returned to France by a laggard steamer called the Théophile Gautier, plying between Alexandria and Marseilles. And back to Paris aboard an express that fairly leaped over the rails.

Two gentlemen from the States were waiting for me at the George V, by appointment. Howard Benedict and Allan Wurtzburger, both of Baltimore, and both travel-minded. Benedict, one of the ablest press agents in all Broadway's history (he graduated to Hollywood and is now a producer at RKO), wanted to go to Monte Carlo. Wurtzburger held out for the Alps. So we compromised on Biarritz. We'd do Paris that night and get an early morning start. Anyway, we did Paris. Right bank. Left bank. Every bank. To the Ritz. And then to Ciro's. And to Harry's New York Bar and the Folies-Bergère and to Le Perroquet and the Dome and the Falstaff bar. And, finally, a swing through several of the spots to which Americans don't take their daughters. In the House of All Nations we met a well-known woman writer, just arrived from New York. She was piloting a few friends through places that made them shudder, but places they would not be denied. Yes, they shuddered, and they were very coy, but not one walked out.

The next day around noon a trio of haggard Americans piled out of the George V, into a shaky little car, Detroit-born, and were off for Orleans, Tours, Bordeaux and Biarritz. . . . I reveled in Biarritz. The season hadn't started and we had it to ourselves. We frequented the Casino and the Café Glacier and the Bar Basque, where the cashier, a truly fascinating creature, sat upon a high stool, hour upon hour, in sublime immobility. Her gleaming black hair was slicked back, her face was ghost white, her mouth ruby red. She never looked this way or that. Once or twice she smiled, wanly. But she never spoke. And her expression never changed. Until she had betrayed herself with that first faint smile we were convinced that she was something done in wax. We went to St. Jean de Luz to hear one of the hottest jazz orchestras in all the world, to Dax to see a bull fight—my very first—and to San Sebastian, so picturesque and peaceful and giving no sign of the harrowing years that were to come.

Back to London and to the Savoy. There was a stack of mail awaiting me. A note from A. A. Milne. Another from St. John Ervine. Another from Charles Laughton. And Edith Evans. And Ernest Milton, with whom I'd spent a day at Hatfield. Appointments that were not possible in April could now be arranged. An entire new "London After Dark" series could be done. But I felt that I had written enough, seen enough, traveled enough and certainly spent enough.

I'd sent more than sixty articles to *The Sun*, these pieces totaling well over 100,000 words. Besides, I had booked passage on the *Île de France*. So I sailed. I shared a table with Evelyn Laye, Mr. and Mrs. David Selznick, Jesse Lasky, Jr., Jack White and Pauline Starke, who was then Mrs. White. Evelyn was beautiful but conversation was not one of her gifts. Pauline Starke was in something of a trance and seldom got out of it—it or her deck chair. David Selznick, who had married Irene Mayer, daughter of Louis B. Mayer, was an interesting talker, a fellow with a quick and diverting mind, but if he talked anything but Hollywood it happened when I wasn't around. In the mid-Atlantic, I got the notion for a play. For two plays. One was to come along two years later and result in my being catapulted to the Pacific coast. My writings, aside from newspaper work, have been sparse indeed. I've worked too infrequently. Swiftly when I get at it, but I've been too satisfied with mere spurts. Call it what you like—lack of ideas, fear of disappointment, general disinclination, or just downright South Georgia inertia. But the fact remains—and perhaps I might get some encouragement from this—that every line I've done for stage or films within the past ten years has been bought by Hollywood. Perhaps I should keep pounding away. Maybe that play to be called "U. S. 40" will be worth doing after all.

Miriam Hopkins was at the gangplank when the *Île de France* docked. In that breathless way of hers she told me the news: Her marriage with Austin Parker was working out all right, thanks. She was in "Lysistrata" and she had made a big hit. The movies had been after her, really this time, and Walter Wanger had been terribly nice. How did I like Egypt and did I need any money? "The Green Pastures" had won the Pulitzer Prize and George M. Cohan was reviving "The Song and Dance Man.". . . Did I really think Eugene O'Neill was happy and what did I think of her going to Hollywood? . . . We told the cab driver to take us to the Twenty-one Club.

Broadway's summer of 1930: The temperature must have reached 100 on the sidewalk in front of the Palace. Belasco, his collar wilting, spent his birthday, his seventy-seventh, rehearsing his new comedy, "Dancing Partner," with Irene Purcell and Lynne Overman in the leads. Brady and Woods, always early starters, were getting their new pieces ready. Grace George was still playing "The First Mrs. Fraser" and "Strictly Dishonorable" was continuing its long run. Thomas Mitchell was in "The Last Mile" as a replacement for Spencer Tracy, who was on his way to a fortune on the screen. Billy Gaxton, who knows as many people as Jim Farley does, was playing in "Fifty Million Frenchmen." The late Jack Donahue was in "Sons o' Guns" and the other midtown entice-ments included "Uncle Vanya," "Strike Up the Band," "Flying High," "Garrick Gaieties," Philip Barry's "Hotel Universe" and an item called "Lost Sheep." There were, you see, a lot of shows around in summers of other years. Give Broadway ten shows in mid-summer nowadays and it's more than grateful. With all the world coming to New York (that was the theory) for the world's fair of 1939 a dozen summer pieces running simultaneously was the best Broadway could do.

I returned to find many of the important players of Broadway set for fall productions. Alfred Lunt and Lynn Fontanne, the finest man-and-wife acting team of the cen-tury, were to do Maxwell Anderson's "Elizabeth the Queen." Jane Cowl had acquired Benn W. Levy's "Art and Mrs. Bottle" and Edith Barrett, an actress who is the most industrious of the summer players but who has a fearful time of it in the regular season, had the same au-thor's "Mrs. Moonlight." Joe Cook was down at Lake Hopatcong, N. J. devising lunatic contraptions for his new "Fine and Dandy" (a $6.60 show it turned out to be) and such first-rate people as Eugenie Leontovitch, Hortense Alden, Sam Jaffe and Siegfried Rumann were

being engaged by Herman Shumlin for "Grand Hotel."
Lenore Ulric, having her script struggles and troubles
since her Belasco stardom, decided upon one called "Pagan
Lady" and Ethel Barrymore was committed to "Scarlet
Sister Mary." The Astaires, Fred and Adele, and the late
Marilyn Miller had a new Ziegfeld show "Smiles" and the
Sam H. Harris office, and George Kaufman were talking
to all the good actors in sight—not the stars—about a com-
edy, "Once in a Lifetime," which was to introduce to
Broadway a new comedy writer of rare attainments—
Moss Hart. Helen Gahagan returned from Italy to do
"Tonight or Never" for Belasco. A new dramatist, Paul
Osborn, wrote "The Vinegar Tree" (they never tried to
explain the title) and sold it to Dwight Deere Wiman, and
Wiman, displaying showmanship and having rare good
luck, obtained Winchell Smith as his director and Mary
Boland as his principal player.

I'd done my wanderings and I took the summer and
the sizzling heat without protest and discovered, as you're
apt to, that many New Yorkers, particularly those in the
theatrical business, spend their summers in Times Square.
On the day that the mercury shot up to 99 I called at the
Hudson for a session with William Harris, Jr., of no kin
to the other Harrises, Sam and Jed. Here was a workman
of the theater working at his job and liking it. He was
excited, if it can be said that he ever gets excited, about

Zoe Akins's new comedy, "The Greeks Had A Word For It," and for which he had already engaged Dorothy Hall and Veree Teasdale. Bill Harris, lank, bald, and racy of speech, is a fellow who could match his hit record over two decades with any showman in the business. He seldom struck unless he was sure. Like Arthur Hopkins, his notion of a play to produce is one in which he himself believes. He was behind his broad desk on the second floor of the Hudson, and we talked theater. He never just shuts up as Hopkins sometimes does. Or forgets that you are present, as Lee Shubert can do. Or wander off into hopeless irrelevancies as Belasco always did when an interviewer cornered him. Bill Harris comes straight at you.

Now he said:

"I wonder why I ever produced any plays by Vincent Lawrence. He never made a nickel for me. I guess I liked his writings because he was always so sincere. Funny, but American playwrights seem to go bad after they've had a couple of hits; they get the notion that it's too easy. . . . And about actors. Broadway has become just a Poli stock company. We pick 'em and train 'em and Hollywood gets 'em. There are always good performances being given around here. You seldom see a better performance than that of Mei Lan-Fang. Or Ruth Gordon in 'Hotel Universe.' Or Walter Huston in 'The Commodore Marries.' I like actors. Try to treat them right. Don't think I ever had but one quarrel with a player in my life. That was with Ina Claire when she was playing in 'Bluebeard's Eighth Wife.' She tried to hog the show. . . . 'The Greeks'? It's the best thing Zoe Akins has ever done. Not a line of it has been rewritten and not a line will be. I think it's a swell show and I don't mind Akins knowing I think so. The best play of last season? That's easy. I wish I had produced it. It's called 'The Green Pastures.'"

Richard B. Harrison, the elderly negro who created the rôle of De Lawd in "The Green Pastures," was one of the outstanding members of his race. He had great dignity off stage as well as on—dignity, understanding and kindliness. He'd had an interesting life—bellboy, railway clerk, Pullman porter on the Santa Fé, lecturer on the Chautauqua circuit. He really wasn't an actor at all and had never thought of entering the Broadway theater. He just happened to be in a Harlem casting office when Marc Connelly, author of "The Green Pastures," who was experiencing great difficulty in finding a player for the principal character, saw him. There, Connelly realized, was the man for De Lawd. From that moment until Harrison had signed a contract, which he did with reluctance and only after asking the counsel of many persons, Marc Connelly never let him out of his sight. Harrison played "The Green Pastures" for a full five seasons. Had he lived, the play would have gone on. When he died the play died.

I was backstage during the performance given on the evening of the day of De Lawd's death. With this performance seventy-seven Harlem negroes met the supreme test;
this was the show that was hardest to give. They wept
openly—the Angel Gabriel, Noah, Moses, the Stout Angel,
the Thin Angel, and the children of the Fish Fry. De
Lawd was dead. They knew that they'd never again see
him at his rolltop desk in his celestial cubicle, frowning
and fumbling over his papers; would never again behold
him, as he stood aboard the Ark saying "Dis thing's turned
into quite a proposition," or see him, eyes shining and
face brightening, as he discovered "dat even God must
suffer."

Whatever De Lawd and the others of that remarkable
play did for Marc Connelly as a dramatist and for Rowland Stebbins as a producer, they also did much for Manhattan's Forty-seventh Street. The Mansfield Theater was
a jinx house until De Lawd came along. Once he had cried
"Let de fish fry proceed" in his deep, melodious voice,
boom-times seized the thoroughfare. Shambles to the East
came down and the Hotel Edison began going up. Charlie
Yat Sing flung a new and gaudy sign across his laundry
front. The Gospel Mission cleaned its windows and in-
stalled new chairs. The banjo repair shop renovated and
repaired. The piano store (Mrs. Kramer's) put pink and
green marionettes in the window and crowds gathered to

watch the crazy routine. Two brothers running a drum
shop dissolved partnership and began operating competitive drum shops on opposite sides of the street. And the
Biltmore Theater spruced up and began looking for a hit
of its own. . . . All of this happened when De Lawd
and Noah and the King of Babylon took over the stage
of a theater that had brought only failures to all others,
Mrs. Fiske included.

In a November week of 1930 ten plays opened on
Broadway. Production was still brisk despite the fact that
many of the showmen of the town lost heavily in the
panic of '29. The biggest money-getter of all the pieces
of that fall and winter was "Grand Hotel," which Herman Shumlin, in association with the late Harry Moses,
put on at the National. Moses came into the theater via the
underwear business and, probably to the astonishment of
former associates, demonstrated a proficiency for his new
calling. Shumlin, of Atwood, Colo., with a definite sense
for rightness of a scene or an act or a play, is as outspoken
as managers come. I've always relished my talks with him.
He has now given the town, in addition to "Grand Hotel," such worthy stuff as "The Last Mile," "The Children's Hour" and "The Little Foxes." When he was presenting "The Merchant of Yonkers" in Boston prior to
the New York opening I was with him aboard the Shore
Line Limited, drawing room A. I asked of Jane Cowl, who

was starred in the piece. He smiled, and plucked at his suspenders.

"Miss Cowl," he said slowly, "is a charming actress. A delightful actress. But ——"

And then he buzzed for the porter and ordered another bottle of ale.

It was during that fall, too, that I had one of my many talks with A. H. Woods; his theatrical empire was soon to begin falling apart. He'd summoned me to the Eltinge Theater and I found him in his swivel chair, his feet upon his desk. He blew smoke at me from his cigar as he gazed into the cool depths of his great jade ring.

"Sweetheart," he said, "show business is lousy. I've had two hits this year, but where are they now? You call 'Grand Hotel' a hit, don't you? And maybe you call 'Once in a Lifetime' a hit. I had 'em both but I ain't got 'em. They were both right here on this desk and I let 'em go. Somebody else makes the million. 'Grand Hotel' was mine for eighteen months. Paid $1,500 advance and then I let it slip away. . . . Who is that fellow Herman Shumlin, anyway? Did he play for me in 'The Great Express Robbery' or was he in 'The Yellow Ticket'? . . . Things are bound to get better, sucker. If they don't I'm going to revive 'The Littlest Rebel' with Mary Miles Minter, or put out an all-star cast in 'Ladies Night in a Turkish Bath.'" Cigar smoke now hung in a blue haze about his head but his voice came through clearly: "Watch for that

new one of mine, sucker. It's called 'A Farewell to Arms'
and it's going to be all right."

In the years that I've been with *The Sun* there's been
only one absolutely indispensable member of the dramatic
department and his name is Willie. Just Willie. Few people know that his last name is Priory and there are many
who are constantly calling upon him for services who have
never even seen him. But they've known him for years
and his voice is as familiar as it is pleasant. He's a young
man of broad grin, happy disposition and undetermined
age. He's somewhat bald, somewhat overfed, has traveled
considerably, has a wardrobe not far inferior to Lucius
Beebe's, and he'd rather go to a first night than go to
Heaven. He does go, because he's on all the first night lists
and now and then sits in rows with the critics or even in
front of them. Willie knows everybody and everybody
knows Willie. I've never heard of anyone who didn't like
him. Of Italian parentage, he belongs to a big, active, interesting and voluble family in Jackson Heights. He was
once an office boy on the Globe and worked for Kenneth
Macgowan. Since coming to *The Sun* about sixteen years
ago he has done odd jobs for Woollcott, for Gabriel, for
Lockridge and, God knows, for Morehouse. What others
in the drama department can't do and won't do, Willie
does. He selects all the theater and screen pictures, inter-
views all visiting press agents, keeps track of the film pro-

grams in the thousand and one houses scattered through
New York, and writes screen notes. He is as regular and
as punctual in his first-nighting as Mrs. Ira Katzenberg—
the amazing Mrs. Katzenberg, who pays for her seats,
who is always in the front row, who goes again and again
to the plays that she likes. What would the theater do
without Mrs. Katzenberg? And what could *The Sun* do
without Willie?

It was Willie, of course, and just a little more breathless than I'd ever seen him, who rushed to my desk on a
morning in mid-February, 1931.

"Mr. Speed and Mr. Bartnett are in the hall. They want
to see you right away."

"What about?"

"I can't tell you."

He had a strange gleam in his eye. I went out into the
hall.

"We were wondering," said Keats Speed, "if you could
leave for South America in forty-eight hours."

"I could leave in one hour."

"You can take forty-eight. Better go down and see Mr.
Luxton and get yourself insured. You're going to do a lot
of flying."

Two days later I left for Miami. And within a week I
was en route to Port au Prince, Haiti, on the first leg
of a 22,000-mile flight around South America.

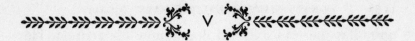

# Below the Equator

IN THE FADING SUNLIGHT OF A BEAUTIFUL SUMMER afternoon—raw March for New York but summer for Rio de Janeiro—the big flying boat which had roared southward from the muddy wastes of the Amazon delta circled the rounded peak of Sugar Loaf Mountain and dropped gently to a landing in Rio's harbor. Broadway and Forty-second Street lay to the north, some 6,000 miles.

Brazil's big. It takes time to get around it, and much of Brazilian coastline remained. Two weeks had passed since the Miami take-off. We had, however, made numerous stop-overs. Pan-American Airways had organized this flight, one of exploration and observation. Spectacular it seemed at the time, but hardly so now with London just a sleeper-jump from Times Square via the Clipper. Pan-American had invited the aviation editors of the New York dailies. None came. My companions on this continent-circling flight were Leo Kieran, *Times* aviation reporter, and W. I. Van Dusen, publicity man for the airline. Van Dusen, a scoutmaster at heart, is now probably far more tactful as a trip-organizer than he was at that

117

time. But the man did, and does, know his aviation. He talked it, dreamed it, thought it, studied it, preached it. He doesn't fly the Atlantic Clippers but I'm sure he could tell the pilots how.

Two great tri-motored Fokkers and two Commodore flying boats brought us to the Brazilian capital. We'd flown over the Virgin and Windward islands, through the Dragon's mouth to Trinidad, past the Guianas and Devil's Island, across the Equator to Para (where there's more rain than Sadie Thompson ever saw) and around the Brazilian hump to Rio. Our guide there was Maxwell J. Rice, young Yale man, who was a manager for Pan-American. He knew all the Americans and most of the Brazilians, knew enough Portuguese to get by, made frequent trips to New York and was having a nice life for himself. He took us to the fashionable Copacabana beach, piloted us along the Avenida Rio Branco, which cleaves the city from waterfront to waterfront, and told us of the ways of the Brazilians as we sat at the Casa des Artes and, from a white-topped table, watched all Brazil go by. He introduced us to canja, for which we were grateful. It's the national soup—chicken and rice. It's heavy with both. And there was another favorite on the Rio bill-of-fares —feijoada. It's an arrangement of black beans and dried meat, stewed together in thick gravy and mixed with rice. The Brazilians eat tons of it and with it they drink caju, the national rum. It was over the second round of caju that Rice, who likes his theater, asked if I knew a New York actress by the name of Claiborne Foster. I told him I did. Well, she was probably his favorite, he'd seen her in several shows, and could he meet her when he came to New York? I promised. Eight months later I introduced them at Tony's. In less than two weeks he was soaring southward with a bride. Claiborne Foster, to her own considerable bewilderment, had become Mrs. Maxwell J. Rice of Rio de Janeiro.

We flew on south, following the coastline. Over the purple plains of Uruguay, across the 200 miles of the Rio de La Plata—which they call a river in all seriousness—and to Buenos Aires for a week's stay.

Jimmy's Bar was on the Avenida Calloa in the heart of Buenos Aires. Blue-topped tables and a gaudy awning gave it the proper sidewalk cafe effect. At a center table sat a great hulk of a man, a fellow with uncombed and overlong locks, great hairy paws for hands, an expansive grin and as slouchily dressed as even Heywood Broun could be. Here was Luis Angel Firpo, the man who knocked Jack Dempsey out of the ring. I had a fascinating afternoon with him. In the Argentine he was, and possibly still is, a god. He'd sit for hours at Jimmy's Bar, sipping his coffee, greeting his friends, and I suppose he must have told a thousand times the story—his own particular

version—of the New York fight that has gone into the
records as the most thrilling spectacle in ring history. "No
push Jack—hit," such is the Firpo version. In the last eight
years his fortunes may have changed—whose haven't?—
but at the time of that Avenida Calloa meeting he had an
automobile agency, he was driving a flashy red Stutz, and
he owned a penthouse, two dogs, a canary, twenty build-
ings and a rancho. He didn't like to talk of his cars or his
cattle. His topic always was fights. He was then some fifty
pounds overweight; he knew that he'd never fight again,
but he seemed to enjoy hearing himself say that he might.
Jim Jeffries kept saying that many years ago and the day
finally came when he did. There are still a few of the
hangers-on at the roulette wheels in the bank clubs of
Reno who can tell you what happened. They'd even tell
you that they saw it happen.

On to Mendoza across the Argentine plain, where the
farms are big and the cattle sleek. And over the Andes,
through the Uspallata pass, rising to 19,000 feet and passing alongside, seemingly, the peak called Aconcagua, the
highest thing nature has devised this side of Tibet. It was
Cliff Travis, a big, blond, likable Texan and Lindbergh's
roommate at Kelly Field in 1924, who was at the con-
trols of the tri-motored Ford on the cross Andes hop—his
112th trip on the route. Now consider that fact—112
times over the Andes, Mendoza to Santiago. Consider his

long flying experience, his barnstorming over uncharted terrain and in perilous weather, his unmarred flying record. Consider all that and you'll fully appreciate the irony of the mishap, a few days later, that cost him his job and that almost cost him his life, along with the lives of eight passengers.

We were homeward bound (and it was all right with me), soaring north from Santiago. It was a beautiful day. The sun was strong. The $100,000 Ford, silver with green trimmings, and considered a wonderful airplane in that comparatively early day of trans-continental flying, roared above the white peaks and every now and then we'd get the glint of the Pacific. More peaks. A rose-water pool, a lush valley. Perfect weather, motors humming, and Cliff Travis was circling for a landing on the field at Ovalle. Then it happened. Travis dropped the big Ford to the flat, unobstructed field. As the wheels touched there was a cross wind and the ship yawed. He quickly gave her the gun, full power, the motors roared, and we were taking the air again. But a wheel struck a fence and a wing tip smashed through a stout stone wall. There was a grove of poplars just ahead; there was not sufficient altitude to clear them. In a tenth-of-a-second decision Pilot Travis spun his ship, then moving at ninety miles an hour, into the ground. It was shattered. Two motors were thrown twenty feet, both wings demolished and the fuselage crumpled. The fact that the nose motor was ripped off undoubtedly saved the lives of Travis and Mechanic Alex Knothe. They jumped. The ship did not take fire and all of us in the fuselage crawled out, somehow. I got a gash in the ankle but wasn't aware of it until moments afterward. Travis, as he gazed upon the tangled wreck of a beautiful airplane, was the most heartbroken man I've ever seen. There were great tears in his eyes as the mechanic picked glass from his blood-smeared face.

Pilot Robinson, of Pan-American-Grace, a supervising pilot in the Chilean area, was brisk, direct, taciturn. He came up from Santiago with two relief ships—a Lockheed and a Fairchild. "Congratulations," he said as he viewed the wreckage. "You fellows were damn lucky; Rockne wasn't."

It was then, in just that way, that we got the news that the great football coach of the University of Notre Dame had dropped to his death in a Kansas cornfield.

We were now shakier than ever. There was night flying ahead, and that wild west coast was not equipped with lighted fields. Panama was five or six thousand miles away. How I longed at that minute for a boat!

Robbie, as his fellow-airmen called him, indicated the swift, single-motored Lockheed, piloted by Harry Colliver, good-humored and casual. Flying to him was just a day's work. Single-motored or tri-motored, what the hell?

"Harry," said Robbie Robinson, "will take you men on north. You'll have to hurry. The mail's got to go through."

We piled in, Kieran, Van Dusen and myself. Robbie shook hands with each of us.

"Good luck," he said.

The airmen respected Robinson. They knew him to be one of the finest pilots in all the South American service. There was a touch of the pioneer in him; he liked his Chilean flying because it was tough. He'd come back to the States sometime, but he was in no hurry. He never came back. A short time after we bade him good-bye on that field at Ovalle he took off from Santiago for the hop to Mendoza with a cargo of Chilean gold. He rode into a storm and crashed. Months passed before his body and his shattered ship were found, buried deep in the Andean snow.

Northward to Panama: Night flying beneath a full and cooperative moon, the Andes on one side and the glittering Pacific on the other. . . . A landing at Arica by the dim headlights of automobiles. . . . Up the Peruvian coast, over the Inca ruins and to a landing at Lima.

We'd been told to expect revolutionary outburst in Lima at any minute and certainly were not put at ease by our first caller at the Country Club de Lima—a voluble American who'd been in Peru so long he was beginning to think he was a descendant of the Incas. He talked as he sipped his gin and tonic.

"Fella," he said, "I've been down here twenty-five years and I guess I've seen twenty Presidents, a thousand Ministers of War and ten thousand Ministers of Finance. I've seen a hundred street battles and I can lay in the street as flat as a dime. I got all the places marked where ducking's good when the shooting starts. Funny how things go in this town. It will be all quiet like and then all of a sudden things happen. Bullets start flying everywhere. Everybody ducks. The streets are cleared. The storekeepers pull down their sheet metal curtains and the battle goes on. In a few minutes—a very few—the shooting stops, the store fronts open again, people come out of alleys and from under porches, newsboys start selling their papers, trolleys run again—and life goes on just as if nothing had happened. That's how it is in Lima. Everybody's come to look at this revolution stuff as part of the day's routine and the town is full of bullet dodgers. Get plenty of practice. I got so much of it I think I could stand out before a firing squad and wouldn't even get nicked in the ankle."

So saying, he finished his gin, said he'd be back to show us the town, and was off for his sugar plantation.

We found Lima serene and restful and actually preferred it to all other capitals. Here was a chance for two days of reflection. The trip was now almost over. A stop or two in Ecuador, a pause in Colombia, then to Panama, Jamaica and back to Miami. It had not been a tour for political observation or economic inquiry. We weren't concerned with the great trade war being waged throughout the continent, with the Germans and the French, the British and the Japanese, as participants. And the United States, but not so aggressively. We were told vaguely of the inroads being made by the Fascists and the Nazis and were aware that the presidency of a South American country, at the time, was the most untenable of all jobs. But all of that was copy for others who were to come. The idea of our flight was to fly a continent when it wasn't being done as a regular thing, when it presented actual hazards, especially on the west coast. And we came through. At Ovalle I suppose we were pretty lucky.

On to Ecuador and with a new pilot, the dashing Kentuckian, Homer Farris (who was also killed in a crash that same year). . . . More Inca ruins. . . . A great condor gliding below us. . . . Oil fields. . . . over a strip of jungle to Guayaquil, the hat town. . . . A change of pilots, with Dinty Moore, who was on the top sergeant order, replacing Farris. . . . To the fascinating jungle village of Esmeraldas, with thatched houses on stilts, and black men riding about in canoes made from the trunks of great trees. . . . And on to Panama.

We went to the Hotel Washington, Colon. In nearly every important stop around the entire continent—Rio, Montevideo, Buenos Aires, Santiago, Lima—I encountered one or more persons I'd previously known. In Rio there was a young man, then in the employ of a coffee plantation, who had once lived at the Algonquin. In Montevideo an ex-Atlantian was working for a bottling concern. And now, as we stood at the desk of the Washington, there came this greeting:

"Well, how's Broadway?"

It was the night clerk, Ted Dickson, with whom I'd covered the weekly Rotary Club luncheons in Savannah.

"I suppose," he said, "you're going to ask me what in hell I'm doing way down here. Well, go ahead and ask it. And what am I doing in the hotel business? I came down here for what I thought was a swell proposition— growing coconuts. Before long I was out of that and was raising sheep. And now I'm back of a hotel desk. Thought it would be romantic living down on the Isthmus. Romantic, my eye! I'm taking a banana boat out of here next Saturday for New Orleans. I want a job on the copy desk!"

I'd forgotten the cut in my ankle until we reached Panama. I then learned that when they sewed it up on that pasture in Chile a slight mistake was made; the poison, averred the doctor in Colon, had been sewed into it. He did the job all over again, and suggested that the hospital in Miami would be the very thing for about two weeks. I stayed two days, took the plane to New York and arrived in time to see the opening of Fred and Adele Astaire in "The Band Wagon." Even to one hobbling on crutches it was a swell show.

Everybody else was welcome to Latin America for awhile, thank you. To the seas, the mountains, the jungles; to the glories of Rio and B. A., to the Inca ruins and the Panamanian isthmus. And to the airplanes. I was glad to be riding once more on tri-motored subways.

Never before had Broadway seemed so much like home.

The New York theater, that spring, saw the passing of two important and picturesque figures—Joe Leblang, the cut-rate ticket king, who had built a great business from his humble start in a little tobacco shop at Sixth Avenue and Thirty-first Street, and David Belasco. Leblang's widow took his business and ran it. Belasco's death meant the finish of the Belasco production organization. Charles Frohman's name stayed on the houseboards long after he died aboard the *Lusitania*, but with Belasco gone there was no one to carry on. None of his associates cared even to try. They'd all now go their separate ways—Benjamin Roeder, Tom Curry, Burke Symon, Herman

Bookbinder, Arthur J. Levy, Miss E. B. Ginty. They'd have reunions every year, they'd make pilgrimages to the grave, but the firm was no longer in business. When "The Governor's" heart stopped at the Hotel Gladstone on the afternoon of May 14, 1931, the familiar legend, "David Belasco Presents—" was gone forever from the American theater.

Hollywood, which really discovered Broadway with the advent of the talkies, was now relentless and unsparing in its raids on the talent of the stage. Players who vowed allegiance to New York weakened when actual offers came. Of all the stars, only Katharine Cornell has stood her ground. She has cried "No!" in the face of every inducement. It's her feeling that the theater is her job, and job aplenty. She is an ardent moviegoer but I don't believe she has had the slightest desire in all her career to make a picture or to have any connection with pictures. I believe even Hollywood must be convinced by now.

I met Katharine Cornell when she was playing in "A Bill of Divorcement," two weeks or so after her triumphant opening, in 1921. In the intervening years I've had many talks with her, for publication and otherwise. There were talks—these for print—at her Beekman Place home, at the Ritz in Boston, in Iroquois Park, city of Louisville, Ky., and at Martha's Vineyard, where I visited her charming summer cottage, Chip Chop, at the water's edge on Vineyard Sound.

"It's just," she said there, "that I have a job and it's the theater—not the movies. I think that's enough for me." We sat in her one-storied, shingled, Cape Cod house, and she spoke frankly of people of the theater, as she always does. . . . "I saw a great Lady Macbeth in London. It was Judith Anderson. . . . I'm always looking for an American play—where is one? . . . I've always had great admiration for Tallulah Bankhead. . . . Sam Behrman is a darling person—so understanding and reasonable. . . . I think Richard Lockridge is one of the soundest of the critics—a man with great discernment. . . . Margalo Gillmore is a fine actress. She and I have been close friends for a long time. . . . My world tour? I wanted so very much to do it. It seems now that it will have to wait such a long time. . . . Guthrie and I would like to do 'Antony and Cleopatra' some time. Why does that play always have to fail?"

Alice Brady went west. Also Claudette Colbert, Fay Bainter, Fred Astaire, Clark Gable, Ginger Rogers, Spencer Tracy, Bette Davis. Miriam Hopkins's offer came from Paramount. And when she signed her contract she recalled that Otto Kahn had once offered to bet her that she'd give up Broadway for the films—at least temporarily. Her experience in borrowing money (which she paid back) from Otto Kahn belongs, of course, to this chronicle. There was the afternoon when she came to the

*Sun* office in great excitement. She had a taxi waiting, was in a hurry and wanted to use the phone. She got Kuhn, Loeb & Co. . . . Mr. Kahn, please. . . . Yes, thank you. . . . Mr. Kahn? How did he do? Would he be there for a few minutes? That was fine. She'd be right down. She hung up. "I've got to have $1,500," she said. "I need some clothes and a lot of things. I met Mr. Kahn at a party. He was nice. I'm going to ask him to lend it to me. I believe he will. . . . Stay here and I'll come back and pick you up." She was back in half an hour with Otto Kahn's check. "He wouldn't give me but $1,250," she said. "I'll buy a drink. I still have that cab outside."

She went to Hollywood—one of those long-term contracts with all that option business and she wrote frequently during the first few weeks. Then the letters eased off and finally they just stopped. That happens to you in California. You quit writing to the East. You even forget there is an East. That wall of the Sierras shuts you in. And most of the people to whom you might write are in California anyway.

The interesting reactions of a young New York actress on arrival on the coast were presented in one of Miriam Hopkins's early letters, written when she hadn't been on the ground for more than a week.

"Well, I'm here. I never knew sunshine could be so gloomy, or people so funny, or architecture so grotesque.

—— has an Italian villa glued to the side of a mountain with two dining rooms and five baths and one of those cathedral effects for a living room. Every time I enter I feel like dropping to my knees and saying prayers. There are forty-three electric lights in the living room (I just counted them). Every time I see them lit I think of Bee Lillie's line when she was riding up on the hill and looked down at all the Hollywood lights and said: 'Yes, they're beautiful but I can't help thinking some day they'll all run together and spell Marion Davies.'

"I haven't been to the studio yet. Nobody seems interested. They called up and said greetings but fortunately I wasn't in and I've forgotten to call back. The pay checks continue every week plus two hundred extra for California expenses. . . .

"That young actor we were talking about is a great success and is going to live here forever. He owns one polo pony, a darling brownish one, and is buying four more. Every afternoon John Cromwell, Jimmie Gleason, Will Rogers (what is the matter with this typewriter? It must have gone Hollywood like its owner) and a bunch of them play polo at the country club. The house—pardon, villa— is filled with mallets, helmets, etc. Then, of course, there is the tennis and the golf—oh, we're just too sporty for words.

"The other day I went to a typical beach party. A little

French girl named —— slapped ——'s face five times. He picked her up by the seat of the pants and threw her out of the house on the beach, —— sat about in nothing but trunks, tiny ones, and he has five rolls of fat about his middle. He helped give Mamoulian a swimming lesson. Mamoulian is going back in a couple of months to direct a play. He is interested in three. One is the something or other in Vienna that the Lunts are going to do and one is a new one by Sam Behrman. And at that beach party June Walker sat around looking healthy and feeling frail. Jeffrey (Geoffrey Kerr) came in from tennis and was very attentive. They call each other Lovey. After supper we wandered over to Selznick's and sat down in the private bar. Sam Behrman said he's going back soon. Dashiell Hammett, long and slim with silvery gray hair, sat about all evening but I never heard him speak. They call him Dash.

"—— flirted all evening with a cute little trick who was all eyelashes. In the center of it all were —— and his wife on a sofa with terrified looks on their faces. When things got a little quiet —— rushed out on the beach and rolled in the sand in her pink lace pajamas, screaming at the top of her voice. I went out to her but got bored and left her, but even at the bar I heard her crying, 'I'm a fool, I'm a fool.' The last I saw of her a drunken juvenile in flannels was carrying her out in his arms. He collapsed and reached to open the screen door but something happened and he dropped her. And at that point I fell off the wagon and had a large brandy and soda."

I went to the World Series that fall, seeing the games in both Philadelphia and St. Louis and witnessed a spectacle that probably won't come again in another half a century: Pepper Martin, out of the great Southwest, a man with a beak nose, high cheek bones and comical legs, beat the Athletics single-handed. Martin, the One Man Baseball Club, gave a $4.40 show every afternoon for seven October afternoons and then, with a plug of tobacco in his cheek and a bankroll in his pocket, went on back to Comanche county, Oklahoma, to do a little work around the farm and dig some holes for telephone poles.

Euclid Avenue, city of Cleveland, drew the outstanding event of the fall season. Maude Adams opened at Cleveland's Ohio Theater (no longer in existence) in "The Merchant of Venice" under the management of the Erlanger office. I was sent by *The Sun* to cover the premiere and, if possible, get the interview I'd been seeking all those years. I failed on the interview but the story of her return to the stage after fourteen years of retirement—the reappearance of an actress who captured the imagination of a nation's playgoers and who endeared herself to these playgoers as had no other player up to and through her time—

was an event, I thought, that would have sent newsmen piling down upon Cleveland in droves. The news services gave the story considerable attention but Brooks Atkinson of the *Times*, so far as I know, was the only other New Yorker who made the trip to Cleveland. Alexander Woollcott went to Newark to see the performance because he was then sure, as perhaps we all were, that he would never see it in New York. Miss Adams got some thirty weeks of playing from the revival. The tour was a financial success and she brought memories to thousands who had seen and cherished her as Peter Pan and Maggie Wylie and Lady Babbie. In her playing of Portia, at the age of fifty-eight, she had the same quaint toss of her head as in bygone years, the same lovely lilt to her voice, but she was not Portia. Also, her production was shoddy and her company second-rate. But all of that, it seemed to me, didn't matter. The story was the return of Maude Adams to the theater. It's a story I'm glad to have had the privilege of writing.

I'd been doing what I could with the notion of the play that struck me on the return crossing aboard the *Île de France*. "Foolin' around," as George M. Cohan puts it when he's working on a script, and before you know it he has phoned Sam Forrest to come on over and they've already begun seeing actors. I wanted to present a kaleidoscopic picture of New York, to do a play projecting the full flavor of the city—the din, the tempo, and the tumult. Uptown, downtown, East Side, West Side—a many-peopled play, done in many scenes, with a love story tying it all together. And I had the story—or thought I had. The play I really had in mind is yet to be written. I didn't write it, although I tried. I just made a stab at it, and perhaps I shall try again. This preliminary effort didn't go unrewarded because Hollywood came to the rescue.

I made notes, notes, notes. All the way around South America. Notes while I sat on the veranda of the Queens Park Hotel at Trinidad, while waiting for the rain to let up in Para, while pretending to listen to an address of the American minister at Montevideo, while sipping a Planter's Punch at the Myrtle Bank, Jamaica, and often while flying over endless green cushions of South American jungle.

Eventually, the stacks and stacks of scribblings began to make a little sense and there was nothing to do but try and write the play. At least try. I got up a flock of my Broadway columns in advance and went to W. T. Dewart's hotel at New London, Conn., the Mohican, for an intensive week's grind. I'd heard of plays being written in a week. Didn't Sammy Shipman do it with "Friendly Enemies"? And didn't Paul Armstrong, a representative of the "punch" school of American drama, take all of three days on "Alias Jimmy Valentine?" They gave me a top-floor corner suite at the Mohican, quarters large enough for ten men and ten plays, and I went to work. Page One, Scene One, Act One. I typed and typed and, wearing out three ribbons, breaking down a portable and almost wrecking another machine, New London rented. Furiously, frenziedly, twelve and fourteen hours a day, generally beginning around 8 every morning and working straight through until 2 o'clock. A pause, a sandwich, and at it until 7 or 8 and some days never leaving the room at all. When I did go down to dinner I'd steal a few minutes off to see part of the movie on the corner. But I was always back at the typewriter, or both of them, by 9 P.M. So it went for seven full days and when I climbed aboard the Merchants' Limited for the return to New York I had 150 pages of typed manuscript, whether I had a play or not. Whatever it was, whatever it was to be, it was on paper. It was glib, the talk seemed bright enough, and I thought the story sound enough. But it wasn't until I was away from it for awhile that I discovered that I had a neat beginning, an excellent finish, and no middle at all. This fact must have been palpably clear to the score or more of the people of the theater who read the script during the next few weeks.

I called the play "New York Town." Copy No. 1 went to John Golden, who'd taken an option, paying $100. Golden has always been one of the great business men of the theater. Never a fellow with leanings toward art, never a man who'd fuss with "The Cherry Orchard," and not a

man who has ever done, so far as I know, a fine play. But a
man who's been a success in show business. What else really
counts? Many producers die penniless. Golden won't. He
was a success as a song writer. ("Goodbye Girls I'm
Through.") He'd have been a success in timber or in oil or
in trucking or in real estate. It's been his good fortune,
plus shrewdness, plus showmanship, to associate himself
with sure-fire talents of the theater—Winchell Smith,
Frank Craven and that remarkable Crothers woman, born
in Bloomington, Ill., who began her playwriting exploits in
years before Taft ever made the White House. She has
stuck to her trade unfalteringly, ever since. A bombastic
fellow, John Golden, given to gesture and to posture, but
a man of innate generosity, boundless energy and an
extraordinary instinct for knowing what American playgoers will buy. It was Gertrude Lawrence, of course, who
sold Rachel Crothers' "Susan and God" to our susceptible,
star-gazing republic. Golden knew she could or thought
she could. Without London's Gertie, who should be taking out her first papers most any day now, "Susan and
God" would never have paid its property bills. Canny
showman that he is, Golden had his eye on Miss Lawrence
long before she came under his management. It wasn't all
Noel Coward that made "Private Lives" a solid sell-out for
three months. It couldn't have been all Coward that packed
a theater with that somewhat tenuous collection of one-act

plays grouped under the title of "Tonight at 8:30." No, it was part Lawrence, a large part. The girl could sell theater tickets. And it's my suspicion that J. G., as Dixie French and the others of his office staff like to put it, made a mental note, "Sign Gertie," when he sat next to her at the Dutch Treat Club luncheon not long prior to the advent of "Susan and God."

Anyway, "New York Town," all tricked up in its jacket of cornflower blue, and slipped ever so snugly into its strong manila envelope, was delivered by *Sun* messenger to the John Golden theater in Fifty-eighth Street (the New York theaters, if you remember, were then moving uptown). It went from Jean Dalrymple to Dixie French to J. G. himself, and then, it seems, to Bertram Bloch, Robert E. Sherwood and nearly everybody else whose opinions he respected. Golden didn't care for "New York Town" as a complete play. He liked the writing and some of the scenes, but he didn't want to produce it. He didn't tell me so until his jury had confirmed his verdict. Then he wrote me saying "No" in several thousand words.

And so "New York Town" set out upon what Broadway has come to know as "the rounds." I had no false sense of the script's values. I knew that it sagged in the middle, but I thought that it had sufficient vitality to warrant a production (with an awful lot of fixing) and I was confident of something happening to it. I was bolstered in such confidence by Leah Salisbury, my agent at the time, and from whom I unwisely drifted because I became momentarily possessed of the delusion that agents should own and fly airplanes, fraternize with the film producers at Twenty-one, refer casually to Katharine Hepburn as Katie, and display only tolerant interest in the careers of writers and actors whose film contracts were somewhat less impressive than those of Charlie MacArthur and Fred Astaire. It's the Leland Hayward office that I have in mind. Leah Salisbury is, and always has been, an excellent agent. Intelligent, aggressive and loyal and perhaps I alone, of the many who know her, am aware of her dark past. She was a dancer in "Kismet," when Otis Skinner took that spectacle drama on the road. Now I've told it and God help me.

How does a play sell when you've used up all the managers? (An experience Elmer Rice seemed to be facing with "Street Scene" until he thought of William A. Brady.) Our play didn't sell to Arthur Hopkins. Or to Herman Shumlin. Or Brock Pemberton. Or William Harris, Jr. Vinton Freedley said he thought the dialogue was swell and how about cocktails one afternoon at Chatham Walk? George M. Cohan wagged his head; said he was damned if he knew what it was all about. A. H. Woods said, "Come on over sometime, sucker, and we'll have a talk about it." Rowland Stebbins, one of the more polite of the managers, just didn't make any comment, and his entire staff—Miriam Doyle, Charlie Stewart—was quite vague about it. I'd about gone through the list when I realized that the script had never been shown to William A. Brady, picturesque showman for half a century. One fresh copy of the script remained. It went to the Playhouse. The next morning Miss Healy, who has been there ever since "The Man Who Came Back," phoned. Could I get to the Playhouse that afternoon? Mr. Brady had read the play and wanted to talk to me. Did he like it? She couldn't say. She knew but wouldn't say. So I went to the Playhouse and ascended via that venerable elevator.

Bill Brady had his cigar in a corner of his mouth and his hat on the side of his head. He was glummer than I'd ever seen him and I'd known him for years. He said: "Sit down." I sat.

Hours passed. Hours. He finally spoke. He said: "I've read your play. I think there's a lot of swell stuff in it. But I wouldn't give you a dime for it—not as it stands. . . . But I'll tell you what I will do."

And he told me. "You've got to have a lot more scenes in that show. It's got to be everything there is in New York. I want to see the slums in it and the Bowery and Fifth Avenue and the waterfront and Tenth Avenue and Park Avenue—everything. You've got to get more romance into it, and build up that love story—build it up—build it up."

He talked on and came to his point: If I'd do the re-writing he'd present the play, but it would be up to War-ner Bros. to back it. It was a natural, as he saw it, for New York's Hollywood theater, Warner-controlled. Done on a big scale, with a stageful of actors, and at a $2 top. We talked on. Jake Wilk of Warners' New York office joined the conference. So did Leah Salisbury. Story conference in the Playhouse!

I wrote the new material within a week, about 10,000 words of it. Bill Brady seemed pleased. Wilk airmailed the script to the coast and that was that. Now we'd wait. As we waited I tried to forget the business of being a dramatist and concern myself only with the writing of "Broadway After Dark." What was happening along Broadway, any-way? . . . Leslie Howard came to town in Philip Barry's "The Animal Kingdom." Pauline Lord played "Distant Drums" for her favorite manager, Guthrie McClintic, but it didn't quite come off. Owen Davis, who'd only written 246 plays up to this moment, began his dramatization of "The Good Earth." Billy Rose, not then given to Aqua-cades, and not then demanding that chorus girls swim as well as dance, was trouping "Crazy Quilt." George Ab-bott, feeling a holiday coming on, sailed for Naples. George M. Cohan moved into an upper Fifth Avenue apartment after years at the Savoy-Plaza. Katharine Cornell finished her remarkable New York run in "The Barretts of Wim-pole Street." . . . And so on.

Washington's birthday, 1932, came along. It fell on a Monday or a Tuesday. I'd been planning a long out-of-town week-end. But on Friday preceding the holiday things happened. Arch Selwyn had read "New York Town" and was excited about it. He said he wanted to do it that very spring. He was going to Virginia—taking the train that very minute. Could I come in Wednesday? Then Warner Bros. called. They weren't interested in producing the play on Broadway with Mr. Brady or anybody else, but they were interested in it as screen material. How much? That was 5:30 P.M. Friday.

On Saturday Leah Salisbury and I went to the office in Forty-fourth Street. The deal was closed in ten minutes. Warner Bros. bought "New York Town" for $25,000—$1,000 down and the other $24,000 payable within a week. The picture was to be made immediately. I was signed at $500 a week, plus transportation and all incidental expenses, to assist in transforming the script into a screen play.

Four days later I flew to Hollywood, my first time west of Denver. I was in something of a daze, and was dead weary when I finally arrived at my West Coast home—the Garden of Allah, 8152 Sunset Boulevard, bungalow No. 8.

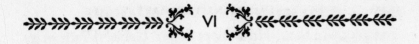

## Beyond the Sierras

TALKING PICTURES TOOK THE ACTOR OUT OF THE $100 class and put him in the $1,000 class. Took him off the Forty-fourth Street curb and whisked him across prairie, sage and mesa to Hollywood Boulevard. Took him out of the Lambs grill, the Blue Ribbon, Ralph's, the automat, Sardi's, Gray's drug store, the Hunting Room of the Astor (very special occasions), the Brass Rails and Ye Old Eat Shoppes and plopped him down in Paradise. Paradise? Well, Paradise to wit: Stuccoed houses, bright tile roofs, swimming pools, lemon groves, flannels, tweeds (imported), rock gardens, wives (new), polo ponies (pedigreed), chefs, Filipino houseboys, built-in bars, bank accounts, desert week-ends, golf, croquet, badminton, roulette, and imported gin. Is it any wonder, then, that once these relaxed and moneyed expatriates get the feeling they're really set that it's difficult for them to leave the shade of the eucalyptus trees? They'll talk Broadway to you until they're blue in the face (or you are); they'll give you the familiar oh-how-I-wish-I-could-find-a-good-play line until they almost have you believing it. But try and get them back! How about it, Mr. Gable? Want to go into a Broadway musical show, Miss Rogers? Care about working for the Group Theater, Mr. Colman? The erstwhile Broadway performers stay in the West because they get big money for doing so. And they stay for another reason. Because they like it. Nobody's fooling anybody any more.

I reported at Warners around 10 A.M., the day after my arrival. I was expected and was told that Mr. Zanuck was ready to see me. Meeting Darryl Zanuck for the first time was like going into the presence of God. He sat behind a gleaming flat-topped desk. Younger and slighter than I had expected. Blond mustache, Walrus teeth, cool discerning eyes, and explosively profane of speech. Cordial enough and I liked him instantly. They were already subjecting "New York Town" to the story-conference routine and I was invited to join in. Robert Lord, ex-newspaperman, quiet and capable, had made a treatment. They were already looking for a new title. Broadway's Arthur Caesar, of loud mouth and savage wit, said it didn't need a new title. "Boy," he bellowed over to me, "you didn't write a play—you wrote a movie. It's a natural. Shoot it!" Arthur's work was done for the day.

There was half an hour's discussion, with many digressions, of the story and the players for it. Broadway's Rufus LeMaire, whose producing career in New York was sel-

dom serene, was doing the casting and the alert Elliott
Nugent, belonging to the practically inexhaustible tribe
of acting Nugents, was to direct. The bland Hal Wallis,
now production chief of the studio, was supervisor. Actual
shooting was to start the instant script and cast were set.
Perhaps within three weeks. Certainly within four. It all
happened just that fast.

Prowling Hollywood, as of 1932 (and as of today) was
like strolling past the Astor during the actors' strike of
1919. Familiar faces at every studio, in every restaurant, at
every party. Particularly at the parties. Faces you hadn't
seen in two, three, four, five, ten years. I've always thought
that one of four things happens to actors and actresses: (1)
They stay in New York and work in the theater; (2) they
stay in New York and they drop out of the theater; (3)
they go to Hollywood; (4) or they die. They don't just
wander off and settle in the Carolina hills or in the Ozarks
or in the Ohio river valley. It's either one coast or the
other. In Hollywood you see those from the Broadway
playhouses who have struck movie gold and those who
haven't, those who are getting rich and those who are just
there. Faces, faces, faces that evoke a thousand memories.
. . . Hale Hamilton of "Get-Rich-Quick Wallingford"
fame. . . . Lionel Barrymore, who was magnificent in
"The Copperhead." . . . Tully Marshall, one of the
pioneers, who joined the movies when Beverly Hills was

just a beanfield; Bayard Veiller, who wrote "Within the Law" and who looked quite unhappy and out of place amid the orange groves; Henry Kolker, who took you back to that sea-going melodrama, "The Greyhound"; Lewis S. Stone, one of the finest players the theater ever lost to the screen. Also, Ned Sparks, of the dry, laconic speech, who made a hit in "Little Miss Brown"; Jimmie Gleason, raising polo ponies; Grant Mitchell, once of "A Tailor Made Man," and now happy with his shack in the desert. Jack Halliday, who liked the West Coast peace and polo. And Edward G. Robinson, one of the best character actors Broadway ever had, and who was, according to Mrs. Robinson, smiling coyly, "on his way to his second million." (Surely by now it must be the third or fourth.)

My first California stay was for four weeks. I was writing extra dialogue for the continuity of "New York Town" and such labors took me at least two hours out of every twenty-four. I went to Palm Springs and to Caliente and to Santa Barbara and attended my share of parties and dinners. There were always the dinners—Beverly Hills, Brentwood Heights, Santa Monica, Malibu. What relentless hosts and homebodies those transplanted New Yorkers do get to be! One of the most gracious of the dinner-givers was, however, a woman who had no connection with the studios—Mrs. Richard Bullen. In her cool detachment, the whole subject of motion pictures vexed her no end, and she saw absolutely no reason for the existence of the industry, but she knew many people of the colony—stars, writers, extras—and she was entertaining constantly. She'd been married two or three times—I believe the correct total at this moment is four—and she'd lived everywhere— Florida, Virginia, New York, the South of France, the Balearic islands and Tahiti. She talked of her life and her experiences, or of other people's lives and their lesser experiences, with frankness, understanding and lively humor. I sought her company constantly, as I did that of Wilson Mizner. He was, for me, the most interesting man I found in all California.

Tall, gaunt, sloppily attired Wilson Mizner, of the Klondike and of Broadway, of Jack's, Rector's and the Metropole, of Florida and the Boom. He was one of the rare wits of the age, and, besides his wit, he had wisdom and humanity. He was a writer at Warners. I saw him daily at the lunchroom, where he generally held forth for an audience of ten to twenty, and several times in the evenings. He liked to go back to the Diamond Jim Brady days, to talk of the Yukon, of Stanley Ketchel and the ring, of Rex Beach, of Bill Brady, of Lillian Russell, of O. Henry, of Wall Street. There seemed to be no phase of human endeavor that his life, which he had lived to the fullest, had not somehow encompassed. And if you mentioned his old friend and collaborator, Paul Armstrong, he'd take out a handkerchief, one that he must have been carrying since the Nineties, and dab at the moisture in his eyes. Surely such a figure didn't fit into the papier-mache environment of Los Angeles county. Stucco, Spanish tile, Japanese butlers, pepper trees, Santa Barbara week-ends. . . . Mizner, how come?

"You're right," he said one evening as he was having Southern fried chicken, California style, in the Garden of Allah's bungalow 8. "You're right. What the hell am I doing in pictures? I don't belong in pictures. I'm a fish out of water. But I'm working. They're paying me. And I'll tell you how I figure it. I look at the whole thing as the shortest cut between here and the grave."

Two months later Wilson Mizner was dead. At the studio we all agreed that he must have seen it coming.

In the Beverly Hills Brown Derby one evening, just before closing time, I found another individual who didn't belong—Eugene Walter. Few people in Hollywood seemed to know him and few indeed knew of his crowded and exciting life. One-time army sergeant and Alaskan prospector, sailor, reporter, advance man, playwright and author of such hits as "Paid in Full" and "The Easiest Way." And here he was in the land of the oranges and the tiled bungalows, a misfit. He didn't care to talk about Hollywood but he did talk, and wistfully, about Broadway.

"Say," he said meditatively, "what's come over New York anyway? There's no place to meet anybody any more. There is no rest, no peace, no leisure. In the New York of my day we made a pleasure out of business. We met at the Astor, the Knickerbocker, Churchill's, Jack's, Shanley's, and now where? There's no place. The only place I know that looks anything like home is that nice hotel—the Astor.

"I miss all the gang around the Friars Club. I miss the boys—Steve Riordan, Victor Herbert, C. B. Dillingham. I miss Erlanger, who always told me the same story all over again. I miss Augustus Thomas. There was a man who broke the trail for all modern American playwrights. . . . And what's become of the glamour that used to surround the actors? When I came to this town there was color to the profession. The actors that you now see around New York are a pretty forlorn looking crowd. They have lost their nattiness."

He sipped his coffee and went on: "How's Frank Case these days? I used to live at the Algonquin, you know. Paul Armstrong got me in there. We had fun. In those days Frank Case was one of the boys."

They'd now found a new title for "New York Town." Sheer inspiration, they thought. It was being called "Big City Blues." Elliott Nugent had been taken off the picture and studio's wonder boy of the moment, Mervyn LeRoy, had been assigned to its direction. LeRoy was as vague as he could be ingratiating, a great man for contacts, and one whose reputation exceeded his talents. The story needed fixing. It needed elaboration. It needed more story. But they weren't worrying, so neither was I. They went ahead and shot it. I went back to New York, returned within ten days and began writing on a melodramatic piece that was to be known as "Central Park." Earl Baldwin was assigned to work with me and Lucien Hubbard was the supervisor this time. Baldwin knew his screen technique, and was, as Zanuck said, "a fellow with a lot of wild ideas and some of them good ones," but he had no feeling whatever for dialogue. Lucien Hubbard, ex-night city editor of New York, is an able producer. Quiet and no bluster. He carried his city-room methods all the way to the gold fields.

As I've intimated, you could walk along Hollywood Boulevard or Sunset Boulevard, Beverly or Wilshire, and you'd be pretty sure of finding face or faces that you'd seen in New York's Forty-fifth Street or Fifty-second. Once beyond the Sierras, New Yorkers had a way of mingling with New Yorkers. Whenever I went to a party it was like attending an Equity mass meeting: John Cromwell, Spencer Tracy, Grace LaRue, Beulah Bondi, John Meehan, Guy Kibbee, Alan Dinehart, Spencer Charters, Charles Butterworth, Eric Blore, Thomas Mitchell, Donald Meek, Burton Churchill, Hugh O'Connell, Irene Purcell, Genevieve Tobin, Constance Cummings (with mother and brother), Betty Lawford, Frances Goodrich, Albert Hackett, Dorothy Peterson, Tommy Jackson, Ruth Weston, Lilian Bond. A pause, and the roll-call continues: Irene Dunn, Barbara Stanwyck, Mae West, Jeannette MacDonald, Rosalind Russell.

William LeBaron of Paramount, when you'd meet him at the races, liked to go into Broadway reminiscences. Edgar Selwyn, who was on his way to being a Broadway matinee idol when he suddenly forswore acting, was, and is, one of the popular hosts of the New York colony. Brother Arch, candid, crafty and enormously amusing, doesn't care about pictures but what chance, he'll ask you, has a man got of making a living in the New York theater nowadays? Lionel Atwill, whom I encountered several times, was a bit on the pompous side; there were moments when he still seemed to be playing scenes from "Deburau." I saw the Nugents and Claudette Colbert and Robert Montgomery pretty frequently; also Joan Blondell and Jimmy Cagney of the dancing eyebrows. When I encountered Tallulah Bankhead, who was there under a terrific contract, she said: "Christ, I love the place. They're paying me. Why shouldn't I?"

Of the many New York-in-Hollywood parties there was none pleasanter than the get-together which was attended by Ross Alexander and Aleta Freel, both young players from the Broadway theater. Of all those present they seemed the gayest and the least likely to be touched by tragedy. They were devoted to each other. Both had definite talent. Both committed suicide.

Maude Adams crossed prairie and mountain range with her "Merchant of Venice" production and opened at Los Angeles's Biltmore. Richard Pitman, Broadway agent and one of my friends for years, was in constant contact with her. He wired me at the Garden of Allah to call at her dressing room after an evening performance. I did and she was delightful. Would I have lunch with her in New York? She wouldn't forget. Mr. Pitman would call me and perhaps he would join us. Miss Adams played her week in Los Angeles, trouped back East, finished her tour in Newark, and went to Ronkonkoma for a rest. And during that summer there came the call from Dick Pitman. We were lunching with Miss Adams on a Tuesday. And so, after fifteen years, my pursuit of her had been rewarded.

There she sat, Maude Adams, lady of the legends, who'd never given an interview in all her life. Time 1:15 P.M. Place: the Colony Club, Manhattan's East Sixties. She laughed gaily, her eyes sparkled, her hands fluttered and she clasped them beneath her chin. She talked of her tour during the melon course. "The tour," she said, "was wonderful. It was thrilling. Twenty-six weeks of it and I was in better health when it was over than when it started. I—

I suppose I was a little frightened when I began. It had been twelve years since I had played and the sound of my own voice had a strange, terrifying effect upon me."

Was touring, I wondered, anything like it was when she trouped under the banner of Frohman?

"Just as exciting," she said. "Not a great deal of difference. Just as uncertain. Touring used to be difficult because of lack of railroad facilities. Nowadays an element of uncertainty comes in because theaters are always changing hands. We played in some strange, quaint places. Some tremendous big houses. The biggest, I think, was in Houston. There I had laryngitis, but they told me it would be all right—that in that house they couldn't hear beyond the third row anyhow."

The robot-like waiter had removed the melon. The erstwhile Phoebe of the Ringlets was now jabbing, daintily, at a soft shell crab. I'd asked about the reactions of theatrical audiences of 1931-32 as compared with those of her Maggie Wylie and her Leonora days.

"They were wonderful to me," she said, and then raced on into quotes: "They often remained in the theater after the performance was over and they waited outside, too. Just like it used to be. . . . We had lots of adventures. In Louisiana we came to a place where the river had just overflowed and the banks had just failed. In a little place called Missoula, Mont., we had to stay for twelve hours—no

train to take us out. The shorter the engagements the better
I liked them. The one night stands didn't weary me—they
were darlings. . . . Indifferent towns? Maybe Denver
and San Francisco. They didn't like us much in either
place."

Her hands fluttered and she clasped them. Her eyes
danced and she gave her head that quaint, familiar toss.

"They were lovely in Salt Lake. Salt Lake has changed
so. It was wonderful when I was there as a child. My
parents loved it. . . . The early Mormons, the pioneers,
were human, simple, spiritual people." She pried loose a
leg of her diminutive crab and took a sip of fruit punch.

Cold cuts had supplanted the soft shell crabs. The animated Miss Adams, speaking swiftly, with varying inflec-
tion, was talking of the plays of her past. "Peter Pan," of
course, was her play of plays. For many reasons. But close
to her heart and high in her esteem stands "The Legend of
Leonora," which the Scotsman finished toward the end of
his playwriting years.

"Sir James," said Miss Adams, "had written a one-act
play with 'Leonora' and when he turned it into a full-
length play he found he didn't care for the last two acts.
He'd come over for it, however, and at a dress rehearsal
Mr. Frohman, Sir James and I were sitting together in an
out of town theater. Mr. Frohman loved Sir James and
would rather have put on a bad play than offend him. We

were talking about the last act. I said I didn't like it. Mr. Frohman protested. He insisted that it was excellent. Then all of a sudden a little voice on my right piped up—it was Sir James. 'She's right,' he said. 'It is a rotten last act.' "

Her eyes danced as she took a sip of fruit punch. She talked on as the waiter served giant asparagus: "I want a new play—something good and modern. I don't think I want to bring 'The Merchant of Venice' to New York. . . . I haven't seen Sir James Barrie in five years. . . . I never made the motion picture of 'Kim' because Mr. Kipling refused to have it done unless all of it were filmed in India." . . . Had she been seeing the plays and movies in recent seasons? She saw "Reunion in Vienna" and she found Mrs. Lunt fascinating. She adored Douglas Fairbanks in "The Three Musketeers." For her playgoing companions she picks friends of long standing. And she then had in her service her two Marys—one named Reilly and the other Gorman—who'd been her devoted companions for years. I told her I was sure that it was one of the faithful Marys who had blocked my entrance when I called at her Atlanta hotel suite fifteen years before.

She laughed softly as she looked at me over the tea roses and told me of a similar discomfiture suffered by Mrs. Nicholas Longworth, nee Alice Roosevelt. Mrs. Longworth had called to pay her respects but found herself denied entrance. "But I'm the President's daughter!" she exclaimed, indignant. "I don't care," said one of the Marys stiffly, "if you're the President himself. Miss Adams is asleep!"

And then she slammed the door.

"Big City Blues" got good reviews from the New York critics; "Central Park" did not. I didn't like either picture. Funny about "Big City Blues." The screen version confirmed all my inner and early feelings about the script. The parts of it that I liked in that suite at the Mohican, as I sat there pounding away with all those New London clocks forever striking, were the parts that read well in the play version and that looked great on the screen. And the film also emphasized the weakness of the portions I'd been doubtful of all along. I wonder if others who have tried to write for screen and stage have had similar experience. Do they walk out on scenes they don't like, with the feeling that how could Mr. Whoeveritwas ever have written such stuff? And do they, with the proper objectivity, revel in any scene or situation that's well done and well played? These are ruminations and conclusions that are pretty obvious but I'll make them, as others are doing all the time, and be done with them. Hollywood, like Broadway, is dependent to such a fearful extent upon the talents of the writer. Seldom can super-exploitation, or even Mr. Zanuck, come to the rescue of inferior writing. What's the use of having a few good sequences or two good acts when the rest of the material falls short? When I try another play, and that will probably be happening any minute now, I'm going to try also to make a rule for myself and follow it: I'll like all of it, all of it, or I'll not go through with it. I don't believe there's any such thing as an author being too close to a play to judge it with any competence. A shoddy scene or an unconvincing situation fairly shrieks at you, whether you're looking at it in the Shubert Theater, New Haven, or in Henry Miller's Forty-third Street, New York. And what's the good of having one act that you're sure is really swell when the next is certain to send you racing to the bar across the street. All of which I shall try to remember.

Traffic was heavy in the Essex House, apartment 3802, park view, during the winter of 1932-33. In the between-party lulls at this Tavern in the Sky, Jean Dalrymple and I collaborated on a movie. It was something for Dietrich or Tallulah Bankhead or somebody. I did the typing and wrote the dialogue, but it was all Miss Dalrymple's story. It was tender and human and amusing and I don't think Hollywood, or one Rian James, ever took bows on the botch that was made of it. Carl Laemmle, Jr. later admitted that somehow, in the process of rewriting and shooting, the original idea must have gotten over to the Metro lot by mistake, for "Bagdad on the Hudson" should have been one of the charming pictures of the year. It was written in three weeks, after the story had been told to Charles Beahan, who was representing Universal in New York. When we delivered the completed script Beahan said: "I think Junior will buy this." And he sent it west.

A week passed. Two. Tallulah Bankhead was on tour in a comedy, "Forsaking All Others," the work of two young men, Edward Roberts and Frank Cavett. The billing read, "Arch Selwyn Presents—" but Arch was merely working for Tallulah. It was her own money, movie-made, and she was boss, as she is of nearly everything with which she is associated (I don't mean "The Little Foxes," Mr. Shumlin). The play had been handsomely produced and extensively trouped; if it stayed on the road much longer it would soon run out of towns. The two badgered young authors, who'd been fighting and resisting and debating and defending and compromising for weeks, weakened in Boston. Broadway seemed doubtful. So their attitude was "All right, get somebody else in."

I got a midday call from Boston. Arch Selwyn and Paul Streger, who was representing the Leland Hayward office (the authors' representative), both talked. Was I interested in an emergency rewrite job? Could I leave immediately? They offered twenty per cent of the authors' earnings, inclusive of screen sale, and all expenses. I took the first plane for Boston. "Forsaking All Others" had a dreary time on the Common and moved on to Providence. I got one complete scene into Act One and wrote an entirely new second act, of which eight lines were finally used. In Providence highballs were served at rehearsals, everybody in the cast took a hand in the direction, and it all looked pretty terrible. I saw just one way of saving the pieces and went to Tallulah.

"All right!" she cried. "All right. Go and get him and quit talking about it. Bring him here. Tie him, kidnap him, but for Christ's sake get him here. I don't give a goddam what it costs. Just get him."

So when I returned to Providence the next day I had Tommy Mitchell in tow. Tommy, now in Hollywood, but an Irishman who will never be able to stay out of the theater, saw the show. He then walked around the block for half an hour before going to Tallulah's suite at the Providence-Biltmore. Everybody was there, as usual. There was never a conference that the entire troupe wasn't in on. The authors, Cavett and Roberts, had been through enough. They thought this was surely the end. Both were on the floor. Tommy had decided to do the job, but he played hard to get. By so doing he put over his terms. What the hell, Tallulah figured, was another $1,000 by this time? Tommy went to work. He was a top-sergeant for three days and rehearsed and rehearsed until nearly everybody collapsed. Tallulah was the hardest worker of them all and never before was so meek. Result: They got a show out of "Forsaking All Others." It came into the Times Square theater and fooled everybody. The company gave a crackling performance the opening night. Tallulah was great. The notices, considering what we'd really been expecting, were excellent. The whole adventure cut deep into the Bankhead savings but she had fun and considered it money well spent.

There was finally word from Junior Laemmle in the West. Universal would take "Bagdad on the Hudson" at $8,000—we'd been expecting more—provided that I'd come out and assist in script revision. We accepted. Beahan sent a check for $1,000 advance and a round-trip plane ticket. I left Newark on the first day of the Bank Holiday and reached Hollywood in time for what seemed The End.

Ben, the one-man bellboy staff of the Garden of Allah, had just taken me to my villa and was bringing in the bags when a picture fell from the wall. Another. A table overturned. A vase crashed. The floor slipped from under us. The villa shook. I looked at Ben. His face was dead white.

"Earthquake!" he whispered, and he rushed out the door.

The Universal lot had a definitely run-down-at-the-heel look when compared with the handsome Warner plant.

And everything seemed pretty vague. Junior Laemmle, whom I've always liked, talked to me lots of New York and Twenty-one and El Morocco, but little of "Bagdad on the Hudson." He turned me over to an unhappy man named Jacobson, who had the rating of supervisor, but with nothing to supervise. Jacobson didn't seem to know what "Bagdad" was all about and wasn't really interested. There was a man named Wyler, however—Robert Wyler, brother of William—who had great feeling for the story and wanted to direct it. He was talented, interesting and pretty screwy. He'd done some directing on the continent but had not caught on in Hollywood. I stayed three weeks, reporting daily at the studio, and we got the script into what seemed fair shape. I collected from Universal, had a good-bye luncheon with Junior Laemmle and took a plane for the East. Dennis King, the actor, was a fellow-passenger on the flight from Burbank to Salt Lake. It was a tough trip. He wasn't accustomed to flying, didn't like it, and at Salt Lake he'd had enough. I decided to stop over and we went to the Hotel Utah, an interesting place, and the kind of hotel they don't build any more. It has great wide corridors, large rooms and high ceilings, like the DeSoto in Savannah. Perhaps like the Onondaga in Syracuse. Dennis King and I talked theater, toured the town, made unsuccessful inquiry as to the location of the house in which Maude Adams was born and were equally unsuccessful in our efforts to get into the Mormon Temple. He got on a train and I went to the airport. Paul Streger met me at Newark with the news that Metro had offered $10,000 for the screen rights to "Forsaking All Others." Not much, but it was an offer. And nobody else seemed interested. I had a vote coming. I voted to grab it. They eventually did.

Two months later I was back in Hollywood, brought out by Junior Laemmle at Robert Wyler's urgings. We worked fiercely on the script for ten more days and it seemed all right. It had story, plenty of it—dialogue, incident, situation. I returned East with the feeling that I really wanted to write for pictures, that it would be pleasant and exciting as well as profitable. And what a shock we got when the story finally reached the screen. It was called "It Happened in New York." It wasn't Jean Dalrymple's story. It wasn't mine. And it wasn't any more like the original than "Anna Christie" is like "You Can't Take It With You."

There was more action from Hollywood. This time from Paramount. William LeBaron wanted a story of the Gibson Girl era, a Broadway story covering the period from the time of Thaw's killing of Stanford White until, say, Irving Berlin's writing of "Alexander's Ragtime Band." Rich, colorful and exciting years in New York. The Leland Hayward office, which discovered every now and then that it had me under contract, got this offer for

me. It was immediate and the money was all right—$5,000,
I believe, for the job. But I had no desire to return to
Hollywood just then. I'd been shuttling back and forth for
a year. Besides, I'd booked passage on the *Bremen* and had
planned a holiday in London and Switzerland. I called
the Paramount studio and talked to LeBaron. He was willing to hold the offer for two weeks, but couldn't for any
longer. I sailed on the *Bremen*.

London plays seemed better. Or perhaps it was because
I was just seeing them, and not seeing them to write about
them. I was taking a leave of absence from *The Sun* and
it was my first time abroad without copy to write. For the
New York playgoer, wandering about the stalls of West
End, things have to be awfully just-so, if he is to like the
London theater at all. It's much easier to take if you're
relaxed. "The Lake," as played by such people as Marie
Nye and May Whitty, appeared to be good drama. Ray-
mond Massey gave a strong performance in a spurious war
piece called "The Ace." Gielgud was in the beautiful but
ponderous "Richard of Bordeaux." Mary Ellis, with something of a West End following, was trying "Music in the
Air" and Ivor Novello, as prolific as Noel Coward, but
without Noel's talent, was doing his latest comedy. I've
forgotten the title. That, in itself, is significant. It must
have been no play at all. For I have always thought that I
could remember the title of every play, the name of every

actor; that I could, without a miss, go through the personnel of the Daniel Frohman Lyceum stock company or the full roster of the original theater in John Street.

Gilbert Miller, who has polish as a producer, who is a linguist and an aviator, and who is becoming, more and more, a showman of the London theater with a branch office in New York, was seldom out of the Savoy grill during that London week. Neither was Kitty Miller, nor Francine Larrimore, Adrianne Allen, Guy Bolton, Florence Britton, Romney Brent, Basil Sidney. Or Dennis King, my old friend from the Utah airways. Marc Connelly, whose stock as a dramatist took a sharp rise with the writing of the beautiful "Green Pastures," gave the best of the week's parties, an affair for Ray Massey held in the Pinafore room of the Savoy. Massey was congratulated on his work in "The Ace." "Great!" everybody said. But he wasn't happy about it. He knew it wasn't much of a play and he didn't feel that he was giving anything beyond a routine performance. He was really getting discouraged about acting anyway. He'd begun to think that he'd have to go in for direction entirely. Some of his friends had been urging him to do Shakespeare; there were others who thought he ought to play Abraham Lincoln, realizing that he could look like Lincoln and that he'd had life-long interest in Lincoln as a character. But how was Ray Massey then to know that Robert E. Sherwood was to come along five

years later with a play that would give him the great rôle
of his career?

I bade Marc Connelly goodbye after that Pinafore room
party, and told him I'd see him in New York. Two days
later we found ourselves at adjoining tables in the Ritz bar,
Paris. These Americans do get around!

A Swiss inn-keeper far down on the Brazilian coast told
me in an evening's stop-over in 1931 that if I ever happened to be near Geneva not to miss the village of Versoix,
a quaint and peaceful place right beside the lake. I'd never
been to Switzerland. Edna Ferber was staying at the
George V in Paris and working, I believe, on the novel,
"American Beauty." I took her to lunch in the Bois, bought
her her favorite wine—Chablis, 1919—and told her of the
European holiday I was having on Hollywood money.

"You're absolutely crazy," she said. Pause. "Absolutely. . . . But how I wish I were doing the very same
thing!"

The Beau Rivage at Versoix proved to be a fascinating
inn. Tumbledown, in need of paint, but spotless. There
were two score cats about the place. Old and young, big
and little, spry and feeble—yellow ones, gray ones, white
ones, and all belonging to the inn's cherubic, apple-cheeked
and madcap proprietress. Shiny-faced Swiss children were
forever pounding up and down the stairway, with a great
Belgian shepherd dog at their heels. One of my two win-

dows was on the street side and after nightfall the continuous beat of feet upon the sidewalk sounded like the patter of soft rain. The other window gave me my view of Lake Geneva. There wasn't a straight chair in the room, but there were two rockers. So I put a rocker beside the lake window, as you might do on the veranda of a hotel along the Massachusetts shoreline, and I rocked. And looked. And pretty soon I'd looked and rocked myself into the first act of a play. I'd call it "Miss Quis" and now, as I gazed out upon the sparkling blue-green of Lake Geneva, that entire first act loomed sharp and clear. I even had the line that would bring the first curtain down. Perhaps I should have sought another lake view, and should have yelled lustily for another rocker, when I began the planning of Act Two.

It was the "Anthony Adverse" era in American life. There seemed to be a copy under every arm aboard the Bremen. The book was all over London. Aboard the cross-channel plane a woman put her nose in it and didn't come out until they shook her at Le Bourget. It was the absolutely necessary part of every American tourist's equipment in Paris. And I saw it again in Interlaken, beneath the arm of a resolute gentleman who had registered from Toronto and who got up at daybreak at Interlaken's Victoria to see what could be done ascending the Jungfrau.

I went back to Paris via Berne and Basle, where I got

my first and only swim in the Rhine, and decided to return to New York via Quebec, the St. Lawrence and the Grand Central station. It all seemed fine, but I had reckoned without thought of the *S.S. Montclare*. There, my hearties, is as leisurely a craft as ever sailed the seas. So leisurely that I feared at times that it had actually stopped in mid-ocean. I sailed from Cherbourg in September and eventually—I think it was along about Thanksgiving—the *Montclare* came in sight of land. Yes, there it was—land! The purplish blur of Labrador from the starboard side.

It was in the summer of 1933 that Winchell Smith, director, author, actor, mill-owner and play-fixer, died at Farmington, Conn. And now, soon after my return to Broadway, Martin Herman died at his New York hotel. Winchell Smith, who began his career with William Gillette in "Secret Service," and Martin Herman of the Eltinge, the one theatrical manager who didn't lie. Both gone. I lost two good friends and the Broadway theater lost two great personalities and two showmen it will never replace.

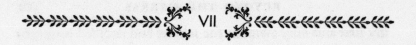 

## VII

## First Nights

ALEXANDER WOOLLCOTT, CLAD IN WHITE SILK pajamas, fretted over his morning coffee and orange juice. He was in the living room of his pine-paneled, second-floor apartment. The East River slid past his big window. We'd been discussing the play, "The Dark Tower," which he wrote in collaboration with George S. Kaufman. There was talk along Broadway of the first-night audience, supposedly hand-picked, that had received the play at the Morosco.

He blinked at me, sipped his coffee, and snorted: "Bloody nonsense. We merely put seats on sale at the box office and hoped in this way to keep out some of the bad mannered element. We were only moderately successful. I reviewed plays for thirteen years and I quit because I didn't want to spend the rest of my life in that company."

Another gulp of coffee and he gazed absent-mindedly out his window. "I own this flat. I like to sit here and watch the big boats and the little boats and the dead bodies go by. Those bodies generally make about ten knots an hour."

A tug churned its way past Wit's End, which was

Dorothy Parker's name for his abode at the waterside. Another tug. A barge and a huge sand scow. He came out of something of a trance and soon was talking of actors and critics.

"Now suppose," he said, "that I'd been lost to civilization for three or four years—say, in darkest Africa or at the headwaters of the Amazon subsisting on wild berries and monkey meat—and suddenly returned to New York. As I came up the bay I would have to decide what actress I'd rather see than any other. Well, in that case, I'd say Ruth Gordon. There's a supremely fine and interesting actress. I like to watch her in the sense that I liked to watch Mrs. Fiske and Emily Stevens. . . . Now, if I had a stock company and had to see this company every day my first actress would be Helen Hayes and my leading man Alfred Lunt."

The ample Mr. W., essayist, lecturer, radio speaker, story-teller, playwright, actor and ex-critic, helped himself to more coffee. He drinks pots and pots of it over his morning's labors. He rises early and generally has three or four hours' work done before any of his friends are up.

He was now amiable and voluble enough as we took up the case of the New York critics: "Why, the critics are all nice fellows. They're honest. They write what they think. But they don't know a god damn thing about the theater. . . . They're gentlemen and an audience composed entirely of critics would be a fine audience, as good as you'd get in a college town. The critics are the only representatives of civilized, decent American life in the first night audiences that we have today."

He paused, chuckled, and chattered on, acridly: "The Barrymore brothers, Lionel and Jack, are going to pieces. . . . I don't go to talkies but I did go to 'Little Women.' The Hepburn girl reminded me at moments of Maude Adams. . . . Emily Stevens had acting genius but she couldn't adjust herself."

Pause. More coffee. And we were back on first nights:

"When you have a play you certainly don't want your friends and relatives at the première. George Kaufman isn't silly about that. He's a terrible audience and doesn't want people in the theater like himself. He hasn't laughed or applauded in fifteen years. . . . Where can you find a gathering as dreary, as ruthless and as moronic as you do at a Broadway first night? First nights have lost their charm and flavor. I never go any more. I simply won't sit in that company. The newspapers have helped to ruin premières and the theaters have let them get away with it. Why, for instance, should the *Times* get six pairs of first night seats? A première night should be a pleasant occasion. It used to be. But now it has become an unbearable one."

When A. Woollcott, pride of Hamilton College, thus

expressed himself I'd been attending first nights steadily for a full ten seasons. Put my total at 100 premières a season, multiply, and see what you get. The first-night personnel seems to change but little through the years. When I'm called upon in the hereafter to tell the court, to the best of my ability, the names of persons seen at première performances in the City of New York, United States of America, I'll go into a chant and rattle off the names unfalteringly:

Mrs. Katzenberg, Hiram Bloomingdale, Jules Glaenzer, William Rhinelander Stewart, Brock Pemberton, Sam H. Harris, Martin Beck, Hope Hampton, Jules Brulatour, Lee Shubert, Bertrand Taylor, Dr. Nathaniel Lief, Margaret Pemberton, Fannie Hurst, Theresa Helburn, Max Gordon, J. Robert Rubin, Bertram Bloch, Paul Streger, Lawrence Langner, Armina Marshall, Franklin Underwood, Jacob Wilk, Johnson Briscoe, John Byram, Bennett Cerf, C. P. Greneker, Bide Dudley, Harry Hershfield, Bernard Gimbel, Lillian Greneker, Kitty Watts, Al Altman, Sam Lyons, Chamberlain Brown, Lyman Brown, Dr. Jerome Wagner, George Goldsmith, Miriam Howell, Katherine Brown, Clara Bell Walsh, Herbert Bayard Swope, Jock Whitney, Bertram Weal.

Pause for breath and then on with it. . . . Condé Nast, Max Dreyfuss, Otto Harbach, Frank Case, Paul Moss, Courtney Burr, Kiviette, Beatrice Kaufman, Nelson

Doubleday, Marcus Heiman, Cole Porter, Hassard Short, Beth Leary, L. Lawrence Weber, Norman Bel Geddes, Adolf Zukor, Dr. Leo Michel, Katherine Forbes-Leith, Harriet Silverman, Leo J. Rosett, Dr. H. A. Rafsky, Fania Marinoff, Carl Van Vechten, Louis Schurr (with blonde), Charles Beahan, Morris Gest, H. I. Chanin, Irving Caesar, M. H. Aylesworth, Lee Simonson, Mary Rockwell, Richard Maney, Erin O'Brien-Moore, Dorothy Hall, Leland Hayward, John C. Wilson, Jules Bache, Tommy Manville, John Krimsky, Arthur Schwartz, Dr. Cornelius Traeger, Frank Crowninshield, Arthur Hopkins, Benjamin Roeder, Gladys Hanson, Arthur Richman, Paul Block, Leonard Bergman, Neysa McMein, Vinton Freedley, Patricia Collinge, Antoinette Perry, Harry Wagstaff Gribble, Peggy Fears, Mary March, Mabelle Webb, A. C. Blumenthal, Owen Davis, William A. Brady, Henry Salisbury, Dixie French, Francine Larrimore, Major Edward Bowes. . . . And only death stopped the first-nighting of such New Yorkers as George Mayer, Joe Leblang, Horace Liveright, Martin Herman, Joseph P. Bickerton.

Dreary? Ruthless? Moronic? The adjectives belong to Alexander Woollcott. During his long aisle-seat service he, more than anyone else I know, seemed to get greatest enjoyment from première festivities. Regardless of how the play happened to go, or how the actors performed, the sage of Phalanx, N. J., could always be depended upon to give a swell show on his own side of the footlights.

The Broadway first-night set-up, as it now prevails, has its interesting and instructive points. When the first announcement of a première date is made the routine runs along such lines as these:

The producer goes over his first night list (something treasured in every managerial office) and sends forth cards, giving name and play, theater and date of opening. Order slips are enclosed with the cards.

Franklin Underwood of Twentieth Century-Fox writes in for eight seats. No check with first letter.

The Sam Goldwyn office writes for seats. No check.

A letter from Mrs. Katzenberg, 270 Park Avenue, arrives. She requests her usual seats in the front row. She encloses check and usually guesses correctly as to the price.

Jules Glaenzer phones. He phones many times. He seldom misses and is seldom late for a première.

Money orders begin piling in, particularly when it's the announcement of a big opening. The producers become wary, suspecting that "diggers" for ticket brokers are at work.

The producer takes a chart of the theater and blocks out the seat locations. Most of the important managers like to attend personally to the assignment of locations. Care is taken in the assigning of seats adjoining those of the critics. The producer doesn't like to put a great laugher

next to a critic. Nor anyone who is likely to be
a friend of the author's or of any of the players.
And a sour-puss is never placed alongside a reviewer if the manager can prevent it. Only
pleasant, quiet people.

The opening night press locations generally run from
110 to 120 seats and the second night "press" goes from
56 to 80. Theatergoers have never seemed to learn that
it's nearly always possible to see a show on the second
night. Complete sell-outs on the second nights are rare.
Even a real smash success often takes a few nights to get
going.

Everybody except members of the invited press pays
for first-night seats. A producer buys seats for his own
show. His author or authors and his players do the same.

Critics, columnists, dramatic editors and others of the
press attending by courtesy of the management are fussy
about where they sit. Occasionally seats are returned to a
press department because the recipient did not consider
them good enough.

The motion picture people, the New York representatives and those in town from the coast, are very sensitive
about their locations. They're seldom satisfied. Nobody
likes to sit behind anybody else. The picture people always ask for more seats than they get.

There are several of the regular first-nighters who are

definitely "front row." They are rarely put anywhere else. Mrs. Katzenberg, the ace theatergoer, is always a front row customer. Others of first-row society are Jules Glaenzer, J. Robert Rubin, William Rhinelander Stewart, Sam H. Harris, Jock Whitney, Bertrand Taylor, Martin Beck, Jules Brulatour, Hope Hampton. Managers don't like to sit Brulatour next to a critic because he never cracks a smile.

There are first-nighters who ask for the last row, so that they can get away in a hurry. Variety often requests back-of-the-house seats. Bide Dudley and Harry Hershfield, both of whom broadcast play reviews, are last row sitters. So is Antoinette Perry.

Curtain-time is often a problem for a manager. All showmen like to start a show at the announced time. A heavy rain at 8:30 P.M. can prove disastrous. A traffic jam in the Forties, one caused by a fire, may delay a curtain indefinitely. Critics are generally punctual, much more nowadays than they used to be, and if a manager says he's going up at 8:45 they take him at his word.

The intermission is always a problem. The great majority of first-nighters leave their seats when the curtain falls. They go out for air, for a smoke, for a drink. Rarely indeed is everyone seated when the show is resumed.

The jitterbug autograph chasers come under the nuisance category. Most managers would like to have their theater fronts cleared of them. When "Stars in Your Eyes" opened seven cops were assigned to duty at the Majestic theater to keep the horde out of Forty-fourth street.

Ticket brokers seldom have first night seats for the big openings. And orchestra seats for the important premières are seldom available at the box office. Any play presented by a reputable management, and with an author and cast of standing, is pretty sure to "go clean" on the lower floor the first night. Balcony and second balcony seats for pre-mières are frequently available at the box office. Occasion-ally blocks of such seats are given to hospitals and depart-ment stores.

Authors and stars are generally heavy seat-buyers for premières. Cole Porter, who seems to know everybody in the world, will try to buy 100 more seats for the première of a show for which he has written the music. He'd take the whole orchestra floor if the management would sell it to him. Jimmy Durante will buy all he can get. And he continues buying throughout the run. Richard Rodgers and Larry Hart are excellent cash customers. One of the most courteous of first-nighters is William Rhinelander Stewart. If he is to be out of town on the date of a play's première he'll write and say so, but will ask not to be for-gotten next time. Chorus people buy seats for friends and relatives and generally ask for balcony locations, which is

all right with the management. Boxes don't always sell
and a management will occasionally "dress" a box, giving
it to people who would not come ordinarily but who are
certain to dress for the occasion.

Some openings are almost automatically "dress" openings. The play, the cast, the theater, the time of the year—
the playgoers take it all into consideration. There are certain playhouses that invariably attract "dress" audiences.
Such as the Empire, the Music Box, Henry Miller's. Gilbert Miller is downright resentful when an audience
doesn't dress. He likes white ties. And from the critics he
at least expects black ones. The critics generally oblige.
Richard Watts, Jr., however, is not intimidated. He comes
in his blue shirt.

Most of the New York dailies get eight seats each for
a Broadway première. Those of the press, other than the
critics of the dailies, who are on the first-night lists, include
columnists, dramatic editors, special writers, reviewers for
news associations and representatives of a few of the periodicals. The *Associated Press, Stage Magazine*, the *Wall
Street Journal*, the *Journal of Commerce*, the *Hollywood
Reporter* and the *North American Newspaper Alliance*
get first-night seats. If you happen to attend the second
night of a Broadway show you'll find yourself sitting with
representatives of such publications as the following:
*Vogue, Spur*, the *Nation, Motion Picture Magazine, Elks*

*Magazine, King Features, Time, Billboard, Zit's, Harper's Bazaar, Staats Zeitung, Newark Ledger, New Haven Register, Times* rotogravure department, *Gotham Life, NEA* service, *Christian Science Monitor, Bronx Home News, North Side News, Theater Arts Monthly, St. Louis Post Despatch, New York Amusements, London Theater World, American Hebrew, Postal Telegraph Guide, New York Enquirer, Daily Worker, Arts and Decorations, New Masses, Baltimore Sun, Boston Herald, Buffalo Evening News, Chicago Tribune, Milwaukee Journal, Montreal Gazette, Montreal Star, New Orleans Times-Picayune, Cincinnati Enquirer, St. Louis Globe-Democrat.*

The personnel of New York play first-nighters changes but little from play to play and from season to season. "Who was at the play last night?" a showman asked the day after an important opening last season. Before I could say, "Well, there was Mrs. Katzenberg," he said: "Wait a minute. You don't have to tell me. I know. I'll make a bet now that I can give you the entire list and I won't miss more than ten names. Now see if I'm not right." He reeled off the list, missing only Mr. Bloomingdale, given name Hiram.

The First Lady of the First Nights is, of course, Mrs. Katzenberg. Once you've attended a few New York premières, you begin to look for her and you always find her, down there in Row A or AA, just below the proscenium arch. She's slight and frail and blondish gray and she goes in excessively for powder and no rouge. She's been first-nighting for twenty years and is invaluable as a playgoer, because once she likes a play she returns to see it several times. Mrs. Katzenberg, born in New York, was Rita Frank before her marriage to Ira Katzenberg. He was in the shoe business but has retired. He frequently accompanies her to the theater. "First-nighting," she will tell you, "is the only thing I spend money on."

And there was the comment, of course, of the Broadway actress who was speaking of first nights and first-nighters and speaking, presumably, for the entire acting profession. "Wouldn't it be perfectly terrible for the actors," she said, "if they didn't see all those same tired faces in the front rows on the opening nights."

In March of 1934 I inaugurated a symposium in *The Sun*, ten-favorite-plays-of-your-lifetime, and ran it for a year. Many celebrated Americans, including some of New York's avowed first-nighters, were called upon for contributions. Three hundred all-time lists were printed. And later, in a Ten Great Performances contest, a little parlor game of recollection and tribute, I sought selections from 150 prominent and more or less discriminating playgoers. "Hamlet" won in the favorite-plays balloting, polling 80 votes, with "Rain," the runner-up, getting 64. Helen

Hayes topped the field in the performances-that-stay-in-your-memory competition. Eighty-one of the 150 lists carried her name. Katharine Cornell finished second with 58 votes. The voting in both competitions seemed to sustain the general feeling of the moment as to both plays and players. There was excitement to be found in watching over the balloting and the reader interest must have been considerable for two thousand and more unsolicited lists reached the desk of "Broadway After Dark."

In the best-plays-of-all-time series "Hamlet" took the lead in the beginning and held it all the way. "Cyrano de Bergerac" was strong during the first few weeks but was no match for "Rain" or for "What Price Glory," which finished third. Not one contributor in all the 300 included the piece which was perhaps the biggest money-maker in our theatrical history—"Abie's Irish Rose." The names of the contributors were names you could put in lights anywhere: Booth Tarkington, Hervey Allen, George Jean Nathan, Geraldine Farrar, Gene Buck, Cecil B. deMille, Blanche Bates, Mary Mannering, Mary Anderson de Navarro, George Ade, Darryl Zanuck, Kathleen Norris, Laurette Taylor, John Dos Passos, Douglas Fairbanks, William Gillette, Ina Claire, William Lyon Phelps, Winthrop Ames, Dashiell Hammett, F. Scott Fitzgerald, Walter Winchell, Zane Grey, Zona Gale, Sherwood Anderson, O. O. McIntyre, Thomas Beer, Don Marquis, Elsa

Maxwell, Irvin S. Cobb, Sinclair Lewis. . . . And on and on and on.

When all the returns were in, the lists checked and double checked, the theater's First Ten, according to that eminent Jury of Three Hundred, ranked in this order:

1. "HAMLET," by William Shakespeare. In the 200 years of New York theatricals this is the play that's had the most frequent presentations.

2. "RAIN," by John Colton and Clemence Randolph, based on short story by Somerset Maugham. Made famous by Jeanne Eagels. First presented at Maxine Elliott's Theater in November, 1922. Revived at Music Box in 1935 with Tallulah Bankhead as Sadie Thompson.

3. "WHAT PRICE GLORY," by Maxwell Anderson and Laurence Stallings. Presented at the Plymouth in September, 1924, by Arthur Hopkins, with Louis Wolheim and William Boyd.

4. "CYRANO DE BERGERAC," by Edmond Rostand. Playgoers of an earlier day associate the name of Richard Mansfield with the Rostand hero; those who didn't see the Mansfield portrayal talk of Walter Hampden.

5. "PETER PAN," Sir James M. Barrie's immortal work. First revealed to New York at the Empire, November, 1905, with Maude Adams as Peter.

6. "THE JEST," by Sam Benelli. Presented at the Plymouth Theater in April, 1919, by Arthur Hopkins with John and Lionel Barrymore co-starred.

7. "The Green Pastures," by Marc Connelly. Presented by Rowland Stebbins at the Mansfield Theater in February, 1930, with Richard B. Harrison as De Lawd.

8. "Journey's End," by R. C. Sherriff, English dramatist. Presented at Henry Miller's Theater by Gilbert Miller in March, 1929.

9. "Reunion in Vienna," by Robert Sherwood. First performed at the Martin Beck Theater in November, 1931, with Alfred Lunt and Lynn Fontanne in the principal roles.

10. "The Cherry Orchard," Anton Tchekov's masterpiece. First done in Moscow in 1904. Has had numerous productions in New York.

In the second symposium, concerning itself with individual performances, vote-getting was easy for Helen Hayes. Her triumph in "Victoria Regina" was fresh in the minds of playgoers. Some list-makers, however, ignored "Victoria" and mentioned such pieces as "Dear Brutus," "Mary of Scotland" and "Coquette." Had the contest been conducted at the height of the run of "The Barretts of Wimpole Street" Katharine Cornell would probably have led the balloting, just as the honors would have fallen to John Barrymore if anybody had gone in for such symposium whimsy during the time he was playing Hamlet. Anyway, with the closing of my second contest at list No. 150, the standing was as follows:

Votes

| | |
|---|---|
| Helen Hayes | 81 |
| Katharine Cornell | 58 |
| Lunt & Fontanne | 52 |
| Jeanne Eagels | 43 |
| John Barrymore | 43 |
| Maude Adams | 40 |
| Mrs. Fiske | 29 |
| John Gielgud | 26 |
| David Warfield | 24 |
| Richard Mansfield | 22 |

Richard Mansfield made the first ten by the grace of a single vote. The older players remembered him as Cyrano and as Monsieur Beaucaire. There was support, as there should have been, for Ruth Gordon, Ethel Barrymore, William Gillette, Pauline Lord, Maurice Evans, Laurette Taylor, George M. Cohan, Emily Stevens and Nazimova. The list-makers linked Maude Adams's name with her most famous rôle, Peter Pan, and the admirers of Mrs. Fiske ignored "Becky Sharp" and recalled "The New York Idea" and "Tess of the D'Urbervilles." There are certain historians of the drama who would be, I'm sure, in sharp dissent.

I was working on the play about Miss Quis, that migratory lady who had her beginnings in the Swiss hotel beside the lake. It was my notion that the one actress in all America for the rôle of Liz Quis was Chrystal Herne. I'd never met her and phoned Clayton Hamilton at the Players for her address. Miss Herne, daughter of the famous actor-dramatist, James A. Herne, and married to H. S. Pollard, editorial writer, was living in East Fifty-seventh Street, near the river. I sent over the script of the first act. When I got to *The Sun* office at noon the next day there was a memo on my desk: "Please call Chrystal Herne. Important. Willie."

I phoned. Yes, she'd read the first act. She didn't just like it; she loved it. When could she see the rest? And when did I want to do the play? And could I come in for cocktails around 5:30 on Friday? And be sure, she said, to get there in time to see the Boston boat pass her window.

Chrystal Herne finally got the other two acts but was keenly disappointed. It was possible, as Arthur Hopkins and Guthrie McClintic both observed later, that there was no way of topping, in this particular piece, the first act. Hopkins thought I should have it done as a strong one-act play and write another play about an entirely different subject. But I kept at it and held weekly meetings with Miss Herne. I shall always be grateful to her for her encouragement and her complete honesty. She stuck to the play, declining other offers, until there just seemed to

be no more hope. Leland Hayward was the first unhappy
owner of this much-owned property, buying it in an expansive moment at Twenty-one. Later, an explosive, ex-
citable and ingratiating little man, one J. J. Vincent,
Vienna born, got interested in my fable of the town
of Fancy Gap. Just why I could never understand. He
wrote a check for $500 and bought Hayward out. Vin-
ton Freedley was next in line. He eventually produced
the play. But there were many harrowing moments between the time of his early enthusiasm at Chatham Walk
and the opening at New Haven in the spring of 1937.

Tommy Mitchell, who was still serving as the drama's
one-man emergency squad, came into the picture during
the time of J. J. Vincent's perplexing regime. Tommy
was to direct and play the rôle of Buster Niles, the small-
town gambler. I saw him daily for extended conferences,
brought Chrystal Herne to his office at the Morosco
theater, and went to Boston with him. He was staging
and playing in a little comedy called "Fly Away Home."
As we greeted the new year, 1935, in the bar of the Ritz
Carlton we were talking about actors, about bookings,
about scenery and how much Donald Oenslager's wistaria would cost for the windows in Act Two. But when
Tommy got back to Broadway in early January he'd
cooled. "Miss Quis?" Oh, yes. Oh, yes. Why, sure, he remembered. That was the one about the gambler being in

love with the Fancy Gap spinster. But Tommy's mind was far away. He might just as well have been talking of "Salomy Jane" or "The Girl I Left Behind Me."

I dropped Fancy Gap for a time. Miss Herne, exhausted by the whole business, and justifiably so, went into a thriller called "A Room in Red and White." It didn't run. For one reason, its principal player, the late Leslie Adams, was near death when he began playing it. It was a play, however, that was worth the doing and it gave a measure of excitement to that season's second half. Leslie Howard scored a tremendous success in Robert E. Sherwood's "The Petrified Forest" and then inconsiderately bolted for Hollywood when the piece was good for months of Broadway prosperity. George Abbott, conjuror from Elmira, N. Y., pulled "Three Men on a Horse" out of his big black hat; Alfred Lunt and Lynn Fontanne tried tropical melodrama with Noel Coward's "Point Valaine" (the critics, I always thought, tore this one apart with too great an exuberance); Clifford Odets evoked hurrahs with "Awake and Sing"; Grace George found a play in "Kind Lady"; the Players decided upon George M. Cohan's "Seven Keys to Baldpate" for spring revival—and Tallulah Bankhead played "Rain." Played it admirably, but nobody came. Perhaps if it could have been revived with some sort of dream cast—with, say, Lionel Barrymore as the missionary, Lewis S. Stone as the doctor and Charles Bickford as Sergeant O'Hara it might have become the rage all over again. But you couldn't get Sam Forrest to admit it. Or even Sam H. Harris. The play's perfect construction was still there; its fire was gone. Nobody seemed to care any more about the island of Pago Pago and the case of the Rev. Davidson Vs. Sadie Thompson. The revival's collapse was something of a personal defeat for me because I'd been drum-beating for it for years. And with Bankhead as Sadie. She took the failure with characteristic good humor. Her attitude was all right, that's that. But what's next?

By now the prohibition era in New York was but a dim memory. It seemed never to have happened at all. The spots that had taken repeal in stride, such as Twenty-one, the Stork Club and Jack Bleeck's, continued on their prosperous way. Frank Case, who didn't sell liquor during prohibition, when everybody else did, was holding his Algonquin clientele. The Algonquin never went in for the debutante trade, preferring brains to breeding, but the Southampton set saw far more of Twenty-one's bric-a-brac and the Stork Club's balloons than they did of their own homes. Sherman Billingsley, Oklahoman of the shy smile, the quiet voice and the just-out-of-a-hot-tub appearance, continued in his dual rôle of Santa Claus of East Fifty-third Street and big shepherd of an ever-growing herd of errant columnists. The *Herald Tribune* staff,

plus *The New Yorker* staff, plus those who drifted in
with the two groups, made life easy in Fortieth Street for
Jack Bleeck, who was now heavier, grayer, mellower.
Ogden Reid, with or without Wilbur Forrest, still drifted
in, and so did Geoffrey Parsons, Stanley Walker, Rich-
ards Vidmer, Ned McIntosh, Richard Watts Jr., Howard
Barnes, Lucius Beebe, Wolcott Gibbs, St. Clair McKel-
way—all the regulars. And, of course, Richard Maney,
king of the Broadway press agents—Maney the unquench-
able, the unsuppressable. And, to be sure, M. Jay Racusin, of the Old Guard, and occasionally with a former
member of the Tribune staff in tow. Rac, as we've always
known him, calls it a perfect evening when he can talk,
and get a listener, for tales of the old days of the *Tribune*
in Nassau Street—tales of Oggie and Macfarland and
Sparkes and Reinitz; of Edwards and McGeehan and Peck
and Van de Water; of the mythical man by the name of
Garet Garrett. Since I came to New York I've met many
people. I've been around. But I have yet to see or to meet
Garrett, who brought me up from Atlanta. I still have
hope.

For some time I'd been wanting to go to Seventh Sister,
the medieval retreat of William Gillette on the crest of
a hill at Hadlyme, high above the Connecticut River.
Few people entered his gates. With his servants and his
yellow cats the distinguished actor-dramatist and creator

of Sherlock Holmes lived as a recluse in his fieldstone
castle—a structure with walls from two to four feet thick,
doors of chopped oak with hand carved latches, windows
of stained glass, an enormous fireplace, and a tower afford-
ing a view of twenty miles of Connecticut countryside.
The master of Seventh Sister was a gracious letter-writer.
I had a more or less sustained correspondence with him
from the time of our first meeting in 1934 until shortly
before he died at Hartford in 1937. His letters, painstak-
ingly written, and done in black or red ink—sometimes
both—were incisive, characteristically laconic and frequently profane. They reflected his precision, his courtesy and his unfailing humor. He gave a promise one
afternoon at the Plaza that he'd have me at Seventh Sister, although he'd made a rule against the press. He put
me off for many months. When he finally yielded he
wrote:

Hadlyme, Conn.<br>Aug. 21, 1935

Dear Mr. Morehouse:
 Sure, you ought to come up here. I will be
very glad to see you. In fact, you have been on
my list for a long time—of those I wanted to get
hold of.
 Tell me about when you would find it con-
venient to come and let me figure on it with
reference to engagements, etc. I have to be in

New York for a few days soon, but we can fix on a day before or after that.

It is rather a tough trip. Takes about three hours or more if you come in a car. If by R. R. you get a train for Saybrook, two and one-half hours (Hadlyme is twelve miles up the river from Saybrook). . . . Tell me which and I will send full directions. My morning does not begin till noon or later (I am still a night worker), so you will not have to leave N. Y. at any ungodly hour.

Sincerely,
William Gillette.

(Of course, any one you may bring with you will be welcome—except a reporter boy who is out after an interview. I am sure you will protect me from that).

W. G.

He later sent a map, done in red and black, which must have taken him hours to draw, and suggested its use in getting to Seventh Sister. The map was perfect. When I arrived he was wearing blue overalls, an engineer's cap, heavy gloves and was ready to take me for a ride on his famous private railroad, his pride and joy, and a thing of his own devising. I piled into a compartment and he climbed into the undersized locomotive, blew a whistle and the train lurched from beneath its shed, off on a three-mile journey over the winding, narrow-gauge track. The little locomotive chugged uphill and down, moving at twenty miles an hour and careening over high trestles, through tunnels, and past great thickets of oak, ash, beech, white birch and hemlock. We returned to the "station" on schedule. Then my 80-year-old engineer climbed nimbly out of his locomotive and went into the house to change his clothes.

When I saw him again, only a few minutes later, the transformation was startling. He'd put on a black suit and he stood on the narrow balcony above the living room. He slowly descended and paused, dramatically, at the foot of the stairway. I've never beheld a figure of greater dignity. There he stood, impassive. He spoke in a voice that was dry, crisp, almost shrill. A spell came over the room. It seemed as though Mr. Sherlock Holmes of Baker Street had slipped, all unnoticed, into the great stone house. He smiled and said that he, too, would have rum with his tea.

It was Takizawa, the butler, who poured.

## VIII

## America: It's a Funny Place

TIME: MARCH, 1936. PLACE: 280 BROADWAY. MY LITTLE black coupé, 8-T 6, was poised for cross-country adventure. I'd been assigned by the *Sun* to cover America, ocean to ocean. The coupé's mileage total was then 7784. Three months later, when it brought me back to City Hall Park, the figures had gone well beyond the 19,000-mile mark.

Nothing impromptu, this cross-America jaunt. I'd had it in mind for years and was just waiting to get around to it. I'd seen the Andes, the Pyrenees and the Balkans, but I'd never been through the Ozarks. I knew Sofia and Naples and the spotless town called Paramaribo, Dutch Guiana, but had never set foot in Little Rock or Sioux Falls, S. D. And now 8-T6 was to take me to the South, the Middle West, the Far West. Anywhere and everywhere between the oceans.

I turned westward in Chambers Street to the river, southward to the Battery, and boarded the Staten Island Ferry for St. George. I'd never tried getting into Jersey that way. The city of Trenton was to be the first stop.

In 12,000 miles of driving I saw America, thirty-eight
states of it, and saw Americans. . . .

Alfred M. Landon sat on the broad veranda of his big
Kansas house and placidly smoked his pipe. Martin Eng-
strom, quiet-spoken Swede of Little Falls, Minn., rested
his arms on his hardware-store counter and talked of
Lindbergh's boyhood. Senator Vandenberg, chin cupped
in his palm, sat motionless throughout a listless floor-of-
the-Senate debate. Marlene Dietrich, in slacks, wandered
unconcernedly into a shabby lunchroom of Yuma, Ariz.,
sat on a stool, and ordered a ten-cent bowl of chile. Alfalfa Bill Murray, clawing his scalp, rocked on the porch
of his rude Oklahoma farmhouse and ranted against the
world in general. George Ade, the Hoosier humorist,
sipped his gin buck in the library of his beautiful Indiana
home and blasted F. D. R. Dan W. Hoan, for twenty-odd
years mayor of Milwaukee, lit his black pipe, and said
he'd never run again—never. State Senator Goldsmith
from the Black Soil district of Alabama waved his arms
and said that continuance of the Democratic administration would send the country into revolution. Garrulous
Bibb Graves, Governor of the same state, leaned back in
his swivel chair and called F. D. R. the greatest man since
Moses.

I rode and I looked and I talked to people. To farmers,
sheepherders, coal miners, gas station attendants, barbers,

mechanics, hotel clerks, tollhouse collectors, storekeepers, hitch hikers, bankers, editors, mayors and governors. And when I was done with the 12,000 miles, and sought to take account of my impressions, I had the feeling:

That Roosevelt was the great national hero.

That the Roosevelt following among the people "below the status of hotel clerk," as a Carolina politician put it, would keep him in the White House for a second and possibly a third term.

That the country was one of vast, surging discontent, despite the phantom prosperity then existing.

That editors generally were the friendliest people in the world. And the most optimistic.

That America, despite the WPA construction-signs everywhere, was a land of never-ceasing detours.

That Washington was the country's most beautiful city and that Yemassee, S. C., its most fascinating village.

That O. O. McIntyre and Winchell and others of the syndicated columns were heroes to the millions of the midlands and that the question then most often asked a visiting New Yorker was, "What's O. O. McIntyre really like, anyway?"

And, finally, that our country is big—and it's funny. It's a land of neon lights and chop suey, of Gideon Bibles and overnight cabins. Bank Nights, Pal Nights and Penny Suppers. Roadside zoos, home-cooked meals, porch swings and "666" for colds and fever. It's a paradise of roadside legends: Tourists Accommodated, Good Eats, Honey for Sale, Bar-B-Q, Tasty Foods. It's a country that immortalizes the hot dog, Virginia ham, chicken dinners and the radio. The zoo woman on the Arizona desert whistled "Cheek to Cheek" and the lady barber of Valliant, Okla., hummed "Moon Over Miami" while she worked.

And that was America of just three years ago. Has it changed greatly since 1936?

I went Southward. Camden, a name in the history books and a place of those countless traffic circles. The Pennsville ferry, which has the roadside billing of Ringling Brothers and which takes you across the Delaware. Elkton, the marrying town, on U. S. 40, with so many neons it's like a town on fire. Baltimore, a nightmare of white scrubbed steps and red bricks, house after house, row upon row. Washington, and the cherry blossoms and the crocuses and the senators and the embassies. Alexandria, where the South begins. Along Route 1 to Richmond, where you get the first full feel of it. Raleigh, a stop-over town for the North-South motorists. And on deep into the Carolinas.

Smoke curling from the farmhouses. Sawmills, tumble-down white churches with the paint peeling, stout smoke houses, country ham, old Fords, older oxen, fresh but-

termilk, hot biscuits, fried chicken. . . . Parting sally of
the shopkeepers: "Don't forget to come back and see us."
Carolina wisecrack: "Why, mister, you're just as crazy
as you look!"

Into Columbia, S. C. on a Saturday night. Fords with
muddy and dented fenders parked at the curb. Bustle in
the barber shops, the cafés and the while-U-wait pressing
establishments. Boys in clusters on the corners. Girls
strolling together, self-consciously, arms entwined, and in
groups of threes, fours, fives. Big crush in the corner drug
store, where the soda dispenser—this one's name was
Hap—knows every name, every face, every voice. . . .
"Howdy, what's yours? . . . "Dope an' lime?" . . . "Hi,
fella; make it a black and white." . . . "Dope an' lime."
. . . "Dope an' ammonia." . . . "'Lo there, Betty Lou."
. . . "Why, mister, you're as crazy as you look." . . .
"Ain't going no place—just ridin'." . . . "Come back 'n
see us." . . . "Hi ya, Hap?" . . . "Hi, Bill. . . ." "'Lo
there, Mary Liz." . . . "Dope 'n lime." . . . "Chocolate
malted." . . . "Banana split . . . make it two!" . . . The
radio: "Dinah, sweetest girl in Carolina!" . . .

Momentary hush. A tall, white-mustached silver-
haired man enters. Necks craned, whispers. Then: "Hi,
there, Colonel Blease." . . . "Hi, Governor." . . . "How
you doin', Colonel?" . . . Cole Blease, one of the fabu-
lous figures in American politics, twice a governor, once

a mayor, once a senator and beaten more times than he can remember. Blustering, prejudiced, preposterous, fanatical, picturesque—a creature out of southern fiction of long ago. Lives alone in a great white house, sleeps in a vast oak bed, keeps a jug of corn in a cabinet, two loaded revolvers in the drawer of the night table, double-barreled shot gun, buckshot loaded, over in a corner and Bibles, silver platters and trophies all over the place. Somebody out of T. S. Stribling, somebody who might never have lived at all, but who has, and with great capacity for life.

On into the South. Tatters of circus twenty-four sheets fluttering from barns and stores. Wabbly, two-wheeled carts. Livestock on the highways. Negroes sprawling in the sun. Languor, heat and the fragrance of the tall pines. Great oaks and low hanging gray moss. Azaleas, hydrangeas, weeping willows along the banks of swift, muddy streams. Dogwood ablaze in white-petaled splendor. . . . Towns of the South: Society Hill, Kitty Hawk, Ty Ty, Duck, Skinquarter, Wren, and Bear Wallow. . . . Across Georgia, Alabama-bound. A pause at Macon, where, in a supposedly dry town, the Hotel Dempsey's swing band blared away. Noontime cocktail hour. On, and ramblingly, to Scottsboro, Ala., which broke into the headlines of a nation because a freight train happened to pull up alongside a watertank just beyond town. Nine negroes were hauled off, locked up and charged with the rape of two white women. Take any Southern county seat with the courthouse in the center of the public square, toss in a feed store, add the Cinderella Beauty Shop and the Bocanita film parlor, bring the population up to around 3,000 and you have Scottsboro, Ala., which is now glad to be out of the headlines.

I happened upon Daniel Frohman in Montgomery, wandering along Main Street and seeming completely lost. In Nashville I talked politics with the go-getting publisher, Jimmy Stahlman, of the *Nashville Banner*. In Memphis I encountered Broadway in the lobby of the Peabody: Judith Anderson and Helen Menken, trouping in "The Old Maid" and having a great time. I crossed the Mississippi into the black loam country of Arkansas, skirted the Ozarks, went on up into Missouri, across into Kansas and then into Oklahoma, where I was content to stay.

In Oklahoma it's oil. Indians, yes. And mustangs and poultry farms and great pecan groves and cattle ranches and cotton, but above all else it's oil, oil, oil. You get a surge of excitement as you drive in upon Oklahoma City from the north for the oil fields are crowding in upon the state capitol. The approach is over ground that is incredibly astir. Great clusters of towering derricks right there at the Capitol steps. Hordes of men shuffling about. Rig-builders, tool-dressers, foremen, sub-foremen, muleskinners, roustabouts. I went on into the city and out across the state through the Washita River valley, flat as the floor and rich in alfalfa, barley, wheat, rye. And oil. For miles and miles there were those great clusters of derricks and storage tanks and frequently, rising starkly from the plain, a lone derrick, the wildcat well of an operator taking a chance and taking the word of the geologist. I talked to Oklahomans in Guthrie, then rehearsing the surviving Eighty-niners for a celebration of the Run; in Valliant, in Broken Bow, in Fort Towson and Paul's Valley. They said things were prosperous enough, they didn't think much of Roosevelt but they wanted to know who was better. They were praying for rain; all the Cimarron country was drought dry. They figured Alfalfa Bill Murray, their former governor, had a good chance of being elected to anything, no matter when he ran or what he ran for. And they talked oil. As my little black coupé, 8T-6, carried me westward across the Panhandle I kept thinking of the words of Willard Mayberry, oil-operator, editor, rancher, cow-puncher and secretary to the Republican nominee in 1936—Alfred M. Landon. "Shucks," said Mayberry as we sat in the coffee shop of the Hotel Jayhawk, Topeka. "I've been around a little. I've seen some of this country around here. And I say a man just hasn't lived until he's worked about the oil wells. There's no tougher man living than a rig builder unless it's a tool dresser. Put a fellow in the oil fields for a while and when he comes out there'll be something to him. Or he won't come out at all."

I paused at the Broadway Café in a Panhandle town of wide, straight, treeless streets. I got to talking to an oil man, and there were questions about oil that he could have readily answered. But he had politics on his mind.

"I'm from Ardmore, Oklahoma," he said. "I used to live in Blackwell, and before that in Tonkawa. I know Oklahoma. I can recite its history since '89. I know how it feels about everything except politics. I've quit trying to figure that out. But I know how I feel. I don't like the present Administration at Washington—I don't even like Roosevelt—but I can't ever forget about the time those banks were closed back in 1933. I'm telling you, America was in trouble. Roosevelt pulled us out. For that one thing he can have my vote as long as he wants it. . . ."

New Mexico and the Southwest. In Tucumcari I lost $20 at dice but later won $40 over the green cloth at Santa Rosa, where the elderly female hotel proprietor was her own bellboy and hustled the bags. The $20 profit wasn't to be taken out of the state, for it vanished over a private roulette game in Taos, a low-swung village of adobe houses and zigzag streets, a place that seemed to have strayed over from the Mexican border and hadn't been able to find its way back. There were people in

Santa Fé from both New York and Hollywood and for the reason that they'd heard talk about it and wanted to see it. Once they got there they didn't want to leave. I spent two days in Albuquerque. Pretty dull. Isn't that the town where Eddie Cantor got off the streamliner and began selling beads to the Indians? Albuquerque, if famous for nothing else, has that long brick walk beside the railroad tracks and there the Hollywood stars, deluxing it across America, get out and stretch their legs. I wandered into the once famous Bird Cage Theater at Tombstone, Ariz., and when I reached the Arizona Inn at Tucson, that two-skyscraper town down in the Arizona sun, they gave me the bungalow that had only recently been occupied by John J. Pershing. Tucson is one of General Pershing's favorite spots in the world. And Rose Stahl never misses an Arizona winter. Perhaps the General has never met Miss Stahl. When he was an observer with General Kuroki's army in Manchuria she was delighting American playgoers as Patricia O'Brien in James Forbes's comedy hit, "The Chorus Lady."

Yuma, the Elkton of the great southwest, lies beside the Colorado River, unshielded from the burning sun. Many of the New York pretties, finding that Hollywood brought romance along with other considerations, have gone to Yuma, business-bent. The marriage factory operates at top speed. When I got to Yuma one Earl Free-

man, Justice of the Peace, and past exalted ruler of the
B. P. O. E., No. 476, was putting couples through the
jumps. I timed him. He completed two ceremonies in four
minutes. Handclasps, unctuous greeting. A ring. Solemn
wordings. A hush. An embrace. A bridegroom smeared
with lipstick. Shy passing of a $10 note. Gurgles, forced
patter, crumpled gardenias, giggles, thank-yous, God-
bless-yous, and flight through the doorway of the courthouse basement. . . . NEXT!

I wasn't doing Hollywood on this jaunt. It didn't belong to the America that I was trying to see and my
stay was brief. Dave Chasen, that jocose fellow from out
of the Joe Cook shows, was there and planning to go into
the restaurant business. John O'Hara was writing a new
novel. John V. A. Weaver was about, fretfully. Richard
Watts, Jr., was passing through, en route to China. Howard Benedict, getting on at RKO, was buying a house.
Eleanor Garner Lucas Bullen was talking about divorce.
June Collyer and Stuart Erwin were entertaining visiting
Fifty-second Streeters. The beautiful Anita Colby was
around the Beverly Wilshire and so were Bill Brady,
Grace George, Francine Larrimore and others of the New
York contingent. And Darryl Zanuck's prestige seemed
to be increasing by the minute.

Next stop: Reno. I pushed 8T up the California coastline, across to Sacramento, then over the Sierras and into

Nevada's Truckee Meadows. Reno, after six weeks of it, may become a fearful place, but for two days it's fascinating. I saw more mink coats in one evening about the bank clubs than I had in all of the 6,000 miles I'd traveled to this point. Mink from New York, Chicago, St. Louis, Denver, Dallas. When I put my dollar on the black at the wheel in the lobby of the Riverside Hotel somebody said: "Better watch it. I'm playing red." And there stood Margaret Perry of New York. A moment later Millicent Hanley walked in. And then, god save me, Mrs. Eleanor Garner Bullen herself. She was there to stay six weeks and liked it. She was now to become the bride of a Californian, a man named Wilder. He had money, she said. Or she hoped. We all did Reno. Twenty-one come to Truckee Meadows!

I talked with the editor of the *Reno Evening Gazette*. "Don't get the idea," he said, "that just because we're wide open we're immoral or corrupt. Reno would be a good town without the accessories, such as the divorce traffic and legalized gambling. We have our churches and our homes and schools and fine residences. It must be realized that Nevada is still a sort of mining camp—a frontier state. There is an adventurousness about its people. This is from 'way back. People out here are accustomed to violent ups and downs. The mining industry can give us a depression one minute and then give us a prosperity when there is no

national prosperity. Reno is in a fertile valley—Truckee
Meadows. Things grow here. It's a good town. We love it."

Reno, like Las Vegas, is as wide open as towns come.
Its frontier look is part of its stock in trade. The people
who really live there are placid enough. They work days
and they sleep nights. They read and they go to the movies and they rock on their verandas and are interested in
their gardens and their clubs and their churches. They
live as they would live in Fort Wayne or Des Moines or
Wichita. They don't frequent the bank clubs and the bars.
These belong to the out-of-towners. The stay-ups, the
divorce-seekers from forty-seven states, are the night-
prowlers; they give Reno that weary, red-eyed look. Dice
in the hotel lobbies, roulette with the morning coffee.
Rice, roulette, blackjack, faro—the divorce capital at sun-
up. Dude ranches, dust, bank clubs and bars. Bars, bars,
bars. Those long polished ones, frontier style, with the
big gleaming mirrors and clusters of quiet men in big hats.
The automaton at the roulette table spins his wheel and
straightens his stacks of silver dollars. The eye-shaded man
with the bloodless face continues his chant and his quack-
ings as he rakes the dice cubes across the green cloth:
"Same gunner—coming out. . . . There it is. . . . Nine's
the point. Shooting for a nine. . . . Number ten—field
number. . . . There's a three—that's the field again."

Margaret Perry, mink-coated, daughter of Antoinette

Perry, the Broadway director, felt lucky that night. She was well ahead, but she didn't want to quit. She made two tough points—a four and a ten. She was the only woman in the room and a crowd was now watching her. Her new point was five. The man with the stick continued his chant:

"Same gunner . . . five's the point. . . . Six and five . . . who's getting on that field? . . . There's a nine. . . . Field again. . . . Same gunner—shooting for a five." And she made the five. She now had an enormous stack of cartwheels. Probably $200 in silver.

"Better drag down," I said, not meaning a word of it.

"I'm letting it ride," she said.

She rattled the cubes against the board. An eight! Looked good.

The man with the stick was replaced by a fresher member of the staff. His tone was brisker but his talk the same.

"Same gunner . . . eight's the point. . . . Shooting for an eight. . . . Eighter from Decatur. . . . There's a four —the field again." Margaret Perry paused, shook the dice longer than usual and let them fly against the board. Nobody spoke. The men in the big hats leaned over. One cube showed a six; the other a single dot. Margaret's pile of silver had gone to the house.

She laughed. "Well, I'm cleaned out. I had fun. Let's have a drink."

I went eastward via U. S. 40, one of the great highways cleaving the continent. In the region of the Utah salt flats, where the world's speed records are made and smashed, I stopped at a roadside store, no more than a shack. The proprietor was gnarled, aged, affable. He was glad to have somebody to talk to.

How was he getting along?

"I guess you'd say things are pretty good. Otherwise I wouldn't stay in this awful place. We—me and my wife— we're from Ohio. Heard it was pretty good out here and when we had a chance to buy out this place we took it. We're right here on the highway, you see, and we sit here all day and watch the cars go by. Some of them stop. Not so many, but enough. From what we can make out of it, the whole country's gone crazy. Everybody just spends all their time driving back from one coast to the other."

The Broadway Café doesn't belong solely to the Panhandle. I found another in Wyoming, village of Wamsutter, which is on No. 40. Here the proprietor was gruff and monosyllabic.

"What goes on here?" I asked.

"Nothin'."

"Do people really live here?"

"Tend sheep."

"How many people?"

"About forty."

"How many sheep?"

"About four thousand. . . . An' a lot of sheep dogs. There wouldn't be sheep without sheep dogs. They do more work than the herders."

My black coupé had reached the middle of this immense America. I was moving East. The countryside had leveled off and was dreary in its monotony. At North Platte, Neb. I had my first breakdown. A piston job. It took hours and hours and cost $66. So I saw North Platte. It's about all of America that some of the N. Y.-to-L. A. flyers (weekly heading in New York's *Variety*) have ever seen of America. At the Hotel Fontenelle, Omaha, I had fresh shrimp and in Sioux City, Iowa, I dined on chop suey. After thousands of miles and thousands of chop suey signs I finally gave in. There I called on Editor John W. Carey, cordial, breezy and informative. Sure, things were pretty good. Nobody really had any money but everybody was spending it. Country might go to hell but Iowa was all right. The bankers didn't like Roosevelt but the other people did. How was New York and when had I last seen O. O. McIntyre?

Hitch hikers roam our broad land. They're to be seen in every state. They're near the cities and they're on the desert highways. You rarely see a woman. But the males are of all ages. Boys in their teens, men in their sixties. Trudging along, methodically, resignedly, but never despairingly. Moving toward the next hill, the next horizon and the next—what? A pleasant-looking man, shabbily dressed, came up to me in Sioux City.

"Listen," he said, "I'm no bum. I'm no professional hitch hiker. But I'm stranded and I want to get to South Dakota. I live there. I know people there and I can get work. . . . I guess people think grabbing a ride is easy. It's not. I've been right here asking for three days. Everybody says no. They say it in different ways but it means the same thing."

I took him to Sioux Falls, S. D. and was glad to do it. I was making many stops as I went eastward. . . . Sleepy Eye, Minn., named for an Indian, where 8T-6 got stuck in the mud beside a field freshly plowed for oats. It might be there yet if Mr. Bork of the choir of the Zion Evangelical church hadn't come to the rescue. . . . Little Falls, Minn., where Jim Fearing, Chair No. 1, Hotel Buckman, barbered Lindbergh as a boy. . . . Portage, Wis., to look up the late Zona Gale, only to find that she was in New York conferring with Brock Pemberton. . . . South Bend, Ind., where the president of Notre Dame, the Rev. John F. O'Hara, C.S.C., took me on a day's tour of a great university. . . . Terre Haute, Ind., where three-fingered Brown, famous pitcher for the Chicago Cubs in the Tinker-to-Evers-to-Chance era, ran a filling station, Seventh and Cherry Streets. . . . Indianapolis, that beautiful Indiana capital, where you're shown the town by the redoubtable and red-topped Mike Morissey, Police Chief (never in a uniform, however), greeter and guide. . . . Kokomo, which came into American consciousness via the character of Daniel Vorhees Pike, played by William Hodge in that Tarkington-Wilson fable of long ago, "The Man from Home." . . . And finally, via a this-way-and-that route that took 8T-6 over the St. Lawrence, up to Quebec, down into Maine, to the home of Booth Tarkington at Kennebunkport.

There's grace and charm and wistfulness to Tarkington's life at Kennebunkport. There he always spends his summers and the little coastwise village has the feeling that his home is really in Maine and that he merely visits in Indiana. He showed me his gardens, his books, his paintings and took me to the beached packet schooner which he sometimes uses as workshop. He talked interestingly and humorously of people and events in his career; of his plays and his books. Of Alice Adams and Daniel Vorhees Pike, of Penrod and Clarence and Monsieur Beaucaire. Also, of motoring in the Tyrol and of his writings at Sorrento, with Vesuvius gray in the distance. Like Pinero, and like George Ade, he said that he, too, was now afraid of Broadway. "I just don't go to New York any more," he said. "I don't understand it. And when I was last there I just hurried through."

As I bade him goodbye I thought I heard the crunch of carriage wheels in the driveway and half expected to see a majestic vehicle moving toward me with its lone occupant none other than Mabor Amberson himself, resplendent in the raiment of the Nineties.

I closed the "North America After Dark" tour in the village of Bellows Falls, Vt., mailing my sixtieth article to *The Sun*. I drove on to Boston and when 8T-6 rolled up to the Ritz the mileage figures totaled 12,000 for the trip. I gave the car to the doorman, got into a cab, and went out to see Lefty Grove pitch for Mr. Yawkey's Boston Red Sox.

You can take Broadway for just so long at one stretch. If you cover it year after year you have to get away frequently. But upon returning you always have a sense of warmth and pervading hospitality from the whole area, and you're glad to be home. Such feeling doesn't last but it's pleasant for a time. And now, here were the Forties again, just as I'd left them. The Astor, the Lambs, and Shubert Alley. The gardenia peddlers and the bus barkers. The Shubert limousines, Loew's State, the autograph hoodlums, the Penn-Astor drug store, the Algonquin, Kelcey Allen, Jack Pulaski and Zolotow, and Sardi's hat check girl, Rene Carroll, changeless through the years. All the rest of America—dust bowls, salt flats, Arizona deserts (gas, 28 cents a gallon) oil fields, stucco roofs, Sierra peaks—was far, far away.

Just as I was preparing for a splurge of summertime playgoing—Maxwell Anderson's "Winterset" had taken the Critics' Circle prize and Robert E. Sherwood's "Idiot's Delight" the Pulitzer award since my departure—I was again assigned to the road. To Cleveland, for the Republican National Convention. The Democratic convention, which was to come later in Philadelphia, promised little. But the 1936 show of the erstwhile G. O. P. had possibilities of excitement.

Cleveland's delirium was what it had been expected to be. All the features of the great political trained-animal act came off. All the star performers stalked the stage. That is, all but one. The head man, Alfred M. Landon, knew his stuff. He stayed home. He wasn't a speechmaker, god knows, but his political strategy was sound. This pleasant-looking, neighborly, drawling Kansan, who had come from banking to oil to politics, knew that his place during the Euclid Avenue bedlam was in the library of his big house at 801 Buchanan Street, Topeka. To stay home was his own decision, his natural inclination, and his campaign would have been more effective had he often rejected the goading counsel of his multitudinous advisers and stuck to his own methods and reasonings. With Landon snug on the far side of the Mississippi, the other headliners on the bill did their stuff. Borah, Vandenberg, John Hamilton, Colonel Knox. Colonel Roosevelt didn't fit in anywhere particularly but he knew a lot of people and he was very busy. Borah, the most interesting man at the convention, had one day of glory, but he never had a chance. There was something tragic, wistful and quite heroic about the 70-year-old Idahoan who had waited too long to strike for the presidency. John Hamilton, exhausted to the point of collapse, made a great fight for Landon at the convention. It was later that he weakened on his candidate, and realized the cause was hopeless. Hamilton, an egocentric, sharing much of the acting instincts of his brother Hale ("Get-Rich-Quick Wallingford"), would have preferred to have done all the speechmaking after the nomination, all the campaigning, without ever letting Landon off that Topeka veranda. Landon was acutely disappointed with the selection of Knox as his running mate. And the Chicago publisher had been hoping, if he made the ticket at all, to be on it with Vandenberg. As for Vandenberg, he was wary. He was waiting then, as now, for 1940. He was quite at ease and in rare good humor during the Cleveland excitement. He received an unending stream of callers in his red-carpeted, green-walled suite at the Statler. He had not the slightest interest in the nomination for the vice-presidency on the Republican ticket as of 1936. He foresaw his party's defeat and wanted no part of it. If you talked "off the record" with many of the leaders at that Cleveland show you'd hear what you'd heard before: Landon wouldn't have a chance against Roosevelt. But it was Party treason even to think that way, wasn't it? They'd at least go through the motions.

The tumult raged. Bands played. Flags waved. The streets were crowded. The hotels were jammed, with people sleeping four and five in a room. Cleveland cabs made a killing. The bars were stampeded. Famous people were in town just to look on. Brock Pemberton, loyal to his native Kansas, wore a sunflower and represented Broadway. Cecil B. de Mille was on from Hollywood. Mayor Morley Griswold of Reno wandered along Euclid Avenue greeting old friends. And Alf Landon's father, a benign and somewhat feeble gentleman of seventy-nine summers, came on from Topeka and the river Kaw. He had not long to live and that strenuous week must have hastened his passing. But it gave him the greatest thrill of his life. He saw and he heard the Republican National Convention nominate his son, Alfred Mossman Landon, for the presidency of the United States.

This time when I got back to Broadway, which was swooning in the heat, I took the manuscript of that phantom play "Miss Quis" out of the old walnut desk at the Hotel Madison. I was now going to get it produced or throw it away. It had plagued me long enough. It had been written and rewritten, sold and resold, praised and scorned. People who liked the first act didn't like the third (nobody ever liked the second). Managers who thought it rated a production didn't have the money. Actresses who were willing to play it couldn't be sold to managers. I sent it to Maude Adams, via Richard Pitman. Her response was immediate and exciting. She liked parts of it and wanted to talk to me about the rest. We exchanged telegrams, had several phone conversations, and finally she came in from Ronkonkoma for a meeting at the Colony Club. We sat for an hour and more over tea and crumpets and I was so fascinated watching her, the movements of her head and hands, and listening to that lilt in her voice, that I didn't follow everything she said of the play. She'd brought along a scenario which she'd carefully worked out. It was to take the play from the end of Act One to the final curtain. I didn't feel that it was a better treatment than a dozen I'd tried, but if she'd promise to play it, provided she could be pleased with a new outline, I would have been willing to write "Captain Jinks of the Horse Marines" into the chronicle of Fancy Gap, Pop.: 3,000. But no. No, no, no, Mr. Morehouse, dear Mr. Morehouse. She couldn't really promise. Never. (Toss of head, enchanting smile, chin clasped in her palm.) Never, never! But she'd work on it

with me. Perhaps I might come out to Ronkonkoma?
And perhaps we'd get something we both liked. We finished our crumpets. I'd had a delightful afternoon. I'd
see what I could do with the script and her scenario. And
I'd phone her.

But I never got to Ronkonkoma. It was then that Freedley called—Vinton Freedley of Groton, Harvard and
Pomfret, Conn., who played football with Mahan and
Brickley and who is one of the few managers in Broadway's history born to the Social Register. He doesn't
like it held against him. Could I come on over to his offices
in the Alvin Theater? And right away? I went. There he
sat behind his immaculate desk. He had some news. What
did I think of Peggy Wood for "Miss Quis"? I'll now tell
one, I said. The part was written for Chrystal Herne. How
could anyone ever imagine Miss Wood and Miss Herne
in the same rôle? But, he said, Miss Wood had some ideas
about fixing that second act and wanted to come on from
Hollywood and begin working with me immediately. If
we revised the script to his liking, and if we could throw
out nearly all of Act Two and get an entirely new one,
he'd give the show an immediate production, and with
Peggy playing the rôle of the small town spinster who
inherited all of old Colonel Selby's gold. That sounded
like action. I said all right.

Peggy Wood came East. Freedley got us together in

the lounge at the Plaza, and spoke his piece. It was now late January, 1937. He was going to Bimini for big game fishing and would be away three weeks or so. If we could complete the rewriting in that time he'd put the show into rehearsal in March and open in Boston or New Haven in April. Just like that.

We worked at the Westchester Country Club at Rye, N. Y. Peggy, who has two houses, one new and the other old, and some uncounted acreage near Stamford, reported daily at the club. Peggy's father was an editor. Her husband was J. V. A. Weaver, poet, writer and wit, who died at Colorado Springs in 1938. She is a person of charm and intelligence. She had voice and looks when she got her Broadway start in the chorus and she retains both today. She'd rush into our workroom, fourth floor and on the golf course side, breathless, generally hungry, often thirsty, and always in great disarray. Her clothes were ill-fitting and of questionable taste, her hat was monstrous, her shoes flat-heeled and her glasses horn-rimmed. It was my impression of her then, and it holds today, that when she isn't dressed up she looks like an English governess who expects to sit down with the family. But when she fixes herself—clothes and hair particularly—she becomes, definitely, a beauty. In evening dress her loveliness is such as it was when she was playing in "Buddies," twenty years ago.

Well, we worked. I was neat, she was sloppy, but we

worked. And remarkably well together. Not one of the many thousand who had read the harassed manuscript had ever really questioned Act One, so we didn't bother to remove the brass clips. Act Two was the baby. Peggy did most of that and I did most of the third. I discovered that her sense of rightness of dialogue is sometimes grotesque, and that her comedy ideas generally run toward the slapstick, but that she is never at a loss for construction devices. We had some violent disagreements and spells of mutual enthusiasm. We'd take turns at the typewriter. Now and then she'd go off into endless digressions, particularly when we were stopped by a line or a situation, and there'd be raptures about her poor, dear, brilliant Johnnie; about Noel or Donald Brian or C. B. Dillingham or Charlie Cochran, for whom she had great fondness, or Evelyn Laye, for whom she cared somewhat less. And all of this would go on interminably. And then she'd suddenly say, "I'm hungry." We'd call room service and "Miss Quis" would be delayed for another full hour.

But when the *S.S. Whateveritwas*, up from the Caribbean, docked in the North River on a late February afternoon with Vinton Freedley aboard, we were at the gangplank with the manuscript. He was all tan and all smiles. So we'd finished it, had we? Now how was that second act? And what had we done with the gambler in Act Three? And had we been thinking any about actors and now did we really think the play was any good? Yes, yes, yes, to all of it. All right. Fine. He'd read it that night and let us know tomorrow. No, sir! Here Miss Wood asserted herself and how she can do it. No, he'd read it now! We'd give him until midnight. Peggy and I toured the town, the Forties and the Fifties. We looked in on several shows, we went by the Algonquin and the Tavern and Sardi's and Frankie & Johnnie's and rolled dice with Johnnie for drinks. Our appointment was for midnight, in the northwest corner of the Plaza lounge. At midnight, on the stroke of it, Freedley, accompanied by Louis Loewenstein, then his general manager, came into the room. His face was dead-pan. He came to the table, sat, and looked at us, steely-eyed. Pause. Then he smiled. And said: "All right. I like it. We'll do 'Miss Quis.' Who can we get to direct and who'll play Buster? We'll open four weeks from tomorrow night."

And so we did. The Shubert Theater, New Haven, April 1, 1937. There at last, after three years in a desk drawer, "Miss Quis" was on the stage, handsomely produced, with scenery and trappings by Donald Oenslager and with wistaria (at $150 a bunch) drooping at the windows of the old Selby mansion, regal and austere on its lonely hilltop. Bertram Harrison had staged the play. He did many a hit for A. H. Woods when Sammy Shipman was writing melodramatic heroics, when Hazel Dawn was

darting in and out of doors in negligée, when Charles
Ruggles was frolicking his way through farces about
ladies' nights in Turkish baths. He was now, I thought,
old-fashioned in his methods, but he was a fellow of terrific
directorial integrity. As rehearsals progressed he'd find new
weaknesses and he'd always tell Freedley so. I'd been with
"Miss Quis" for quite a time and above all else I wanted to
see it on a stage. So I compromised frequently. And even
then there were moments when the whole project seemed
likely to blow up. Such a moment came near midnight
during the second week of rehearsals. Freedley had been
sitting for half an hour in pained silence in the darkened
auditorium of the Alvin Theater. We were doing the second act. When he could stand no more he rose, strolled
down the aisle and said:

"Boys and girls, the rehearsal is over. That scene is
lousy."

We went to his softly lit, richly paneled, tastefully decorated offices upstairs in the Alvin. Just the four of us—
Freedley, Harrison, Peggy Wood and myself.

"It's no use," he said, "trying to go on with that act like
it is. We've got to get an entirely new middle for the act
or we'd better just pay off. If you think you can fix it go
ahead."

For the next two or three days Peggy Wood and the
company rehearsed acts one and three. There was no more

playwriting for Peggy just now. She was having her struggles with her characterization. I tore into the new rewrite job and called upon Jean Dalrymple for assistance. Without her aid at this point I doubt if "Miss Quis" would have been produced. The patching was done in forty-eight hours and the new middle chunk of the second act was rehearsed. It was a good repair job. Good enough, at least, to keep our fragile craft from going under completely. And so, with an above-the-average cast, with Oenslager's lush scenery and with what seemed ample financial backing (Miriam Hopkins had put in $2,500 and was our ardent West Coast supporter), the play had its New Haven première and came a week later into Henry Miller's Theater, once the home of "Gentlemen of the Press."

I thought Peggy gave a beautiful first-night performance but in watching the playing of Charles Dow Clark—I was standing at the back and vanished when each act ended—I realized that here was not only the best actor in the troupe but the best character that I had written. Here, with the verdict in, I saw one of the play's grievous faults. The small-town editor, Sam Whittle, played by Clark, was really my hero, and the gambler was only a minor participant, if he really belonged to the story at all. It was right thinking that came all too late and my emotions at the moment were probably akin to the surge of horror experienced by Edna Ferber when, with her novel "Come and

Get It" already on the presses, she became agonizingly aware of the fact that she had killed off her most vital character, Barney Glasgow, before her story was half done. This staggering oversight was later corrected by Hollywood. Had it not been done I'm sure the one-time girl reporter of the Appleton (Wis.) *Daily Crescent* would have set forth across the land for the personal picketing of all the film houses in North America. Or in both Americas.

We had a party after the opening. A little affair, costing only a few dollars less than the entire play production, and held in one of the upstairs private rooms at Twenty-one, with Jack Kreindler's trophies from afar—moose, elk, mountain lion and water buffalo—gazing down upon us tolerantly. We drank wine to the long life of Elizabeth Quis. The two-score first-nighters who rushed backstage (Note to aspiring playwrights: don't ever let that fool you!) had been positively breathless in their excitement. And now we heard the soothing words of Bide Dudley and Harry Hershfield, via the radio. Both called the play a definite success. Dudley went on to say that perhaps the Critics' Circle had been too hasty in awarding the best-play award to Maxwell Anderson's "High Tor."

I was standing at the bar with Vinton Freedley. He gave me a funny look.

"I know," I said, "we'll wait. The papers will be out in a couple of hours."

"Have another drink," he said.

The reviews weren't what *Variety* would call "box office." The critics, most of them, praised dialogue, characters and small-town flavor, but they tore hell out of the plot. They were notices that meant certain failure.

And there you have the Broadway story. You might work months or years on a play, spend weeks in painstaking casting, three or four weeks in rehearsal, a week or ten days out-of-town, and give it your full devotion and unremitting care. Then you come to New York and you have one night in which to make good. Just one night. You hit or you miss. The next day's notices tell the story. Almost anyone familiar with the New York play production set-up can make a pretty accurate guess as to the extent of a play's life merely upon the reading of two or three reviews. Or even one. Broadway, in all honesty, welcomes success. Even those first-nighters who come to jeer forget their pettinesses when they see something they really like. If a play is a hit it is acknowledged to be, even by those who had not wished it well. But when a play fails the almost demoniacal smugness of those who had been rooting against it knows no bounds. It's comparable only to the gloom of the immediately bereaved—authors, actors and friends of authors and actors. What a beating friends take when a play flops! They go to the theater in such sweet innocence. Even in cases of obvious and distressing first-night failure friends of the participants seem to sit happily through it all. They get into something of a trance and stay in it until their indignant perusal of the reviews. Then the friends, like the authors and the actors and the backers, slink into hiding and into silence.

There was heartbreaking significance in Peggy Wood's comment when I phoned her at the Algonquin at noon of the day after our opening. She said:

"I'm still in bed. I haven't read a notice. I don't intend to read one—not today. I don't need to. I know. My phone hasn't rung all morning."

"Miss Quis" was published that spring by Random House, Bennett Cerf having been its loyal friend from the beginning. And it was bought by Hollywood. Only seven or eight of the hundred-odd plays produced during the 1936-37 season were sold to the coast. Several companies showed interest in our play during the five weeks' run at Henry Miller's but no offer was made. I was convinced that there'd never be a sale unless it was done quickly and I went to Hollywood. Selling "Miss Quis" had become something of a habit by now. I'd take one more whirl in an old routine. I did the studios. You can't rush them. You have to sound them out gently. Leland Hayward's office reported lively interest at Metro. I did my negotiating at Columbia. A week passed. No action from either studio. I had to get back to New York. Alvin Adams, youthful president of the Western Air Express and bear hunter extraordinary of Idaho's Yellow Jacket mountains, was going part of the way east with me. As for "Miss Quis," the movies would buy it or they wouldn't. Dave Chasen's spare ribs were great, and his nightly crowd was New York company, but there was no need of my sitting around any longer.

Exactly one minute before the plane's scheduled departure from Burbank, Columbia called the airport. D. A. Doran was on the wire. Columbia was making an offer; they'd buy "Miss Quis" at $10,000.

"Freedley," I said, "will think that's a lousy price."

"It's the best we can do."

"Hayward says he can get $30,000 from Metro."

"Do you believe it?"

I said: "It's a deal. I'll confirm by wire from New York."

Alvin Adams had been standing beside me. When we'd been in the air for a minute or so, and had unbelted ourselves, he said:

"Ten thousand dollars. . . . Hell, man, that's not bad. That's enough to buy a good airplane. . . . Congratulations. I'll tell you what we're going to do. We're stopping over in Las Vegas and I'm buying a drink." We stopped over in Las Vegas.

During that summer Vinton Freedley and I went to

Haiti and some months later I joined him and Mrs. Freed-ley—she was Mary Mitchell of Philadelphia—in a trip abroad. They went from London to Manchester for a Noel Coward opening. I went to Paris and we held a reunion in the Rue Mogador for a performance of the new ice revue, "La Feerie Blanche" at the Theater Mogador, presided over by the bland Mitty Goldin. The evening proved to be the most exciting that M. Goldin's playhouse experienced during the entire season.

We entered during the Tyrolean number and were ushered into seats in the second row. Directly in front of us a theater party of three held forth—a woman and two men. The woman wore a dinner gown of navy crêpe, with a tiny lace collar. Her hat was a navy turban trimmed with ostrich plumes of violet and white. Throughout the per-formance she made animated comments to her companions, clutching their arms. All eyes in the theater, including those of the beaming Mitty Goldin, were upon this trio—not upon the play. Later, at the Bal Tabarin, the Freedleys and I had a table adjoining that of the same trio. Before the evening was over we were presented to them.

It was in just that way that I met the Duke and Duchess of Windsor.

IX

# Critics' Circle

OUR BROADWAY OF TODAY IS ONE OF ORGANIZATION. THE
actors are organized. The stage hands. The managers. And
the chorus girls, electricians, treasurers, musicians, press
agents. So why not the critics?

The New York Critics' Circle really got started several
years prior to its actual functionings. The first best-play
vote did not come until the spring of 1936 when the award
went to the rampant Maxwell Anderson for his "Winterset." He won again with "High Tor" and the third-year
honors were taken by John Steinbeck for the writing of
"Of Mice and Men." Seemingly, the least interested of all
those associated with this play was Steinbeck himself. He
never budged from his California valley.

No award was made for the season of 1938-39 because
no play could poll sufficient votes to win. Lillian Hellman's "The Little Foxes" and Robert E. Sherwood's "Abe
Lincoln in Illinois" were the leaders in the balloting. The
Sherwood drama, denied the critics' silver plaque (an as-
sessment of $15 per critic), went on to take the Pulitzer
Prize. It was the second such citation for the lank and

towering Sherwood, editor in his undergraduate days of the Harvard *Lampoon*.

So, after four years and four voting sessions, the New York Critics' Circle is to be accepted as something with at least a chance of permanence, if that can be said of anything connected with the theater. George Jean Nathan, longest in critical service in New York, is president and John Anderson is corresponding secretary. The metropolitan reviewers have taken something of a naïve pride in their organization, although they're all a little amazed that it could have held together this long. Ordinarily fellows of super-sensitivity, and given to sharp disputes, little jealousies and circles within a circle, they've found an approximation of fraternity in the operations to date.

Membership in the Circle is held to a minimum. The tighter, the wieldier, all the better, is the view of the aisle-sitters. The roster, at the time of the last voting, was as follows:

Burns Mantle of the *Daily News*.
John Anderson of the *Journal and American*.
Brooks Atkinson of the *New York Times*.
John Mason Brown of the *New York Post*.
Richard Watts, Jr. of the *Herald Tribune*.
Richard Lockridge of *The Sun*.
Walter Winchell of the *Daily Mirror*.

Sidney B. Whipple of the *World-Telegram.*
Arthur Pollock of the *Brooklyn Eagle.*
Robert Benchley of the *New Yorker.*
Kelcey Allen of *Women's Wear.*
George Jean Nathan of *Newsweek.*
Joseph Wood Krutch of the *Nation.*
Stark Young of the *New Republic.*
John W. Gassner of *Forum.*
Ruth W. Sedgewick of *Stage Magazine.*
Edith J. R. Isaacs of *Theater Arts Monthly.*

New members will be elected. Louis Kronenberger, who does reviews for *Time*, is in line for membership.

The job of critic of a New York newspaper, or of a magazine of standing, is one of the most difficult in the world to get. There are only a few such jobs; there are thousands and thousands of persons who would like to have them and who feel that they have all the qualifications for filling them. Rarely, indeed, is anyone made critic against his will. In the vast majority of instances, the man given such a post has been craving it. And once he gets set it takes death or the disappearance of his paper to oust him. Critics are seldom fired, and only for extreme cause.

Take the roster of the Critics' Circle as of the last voting —seventeen members. It's a membership, considered as a whole, of high competence. Several of this current crop have developed remarkably during the last few years. The majority of those now reviewing for the dailies will undoubtedly continue in their aisle seats indefinitely. They are skilled, intelligent and of high integrity, although no three of them provide the excitement, readability and showmanship that such commentators as Alexander Woollcott, Percy Hammond and Heywood Broun brought to their reviews.

It's my feeling, and one surely shared by thousands of followers of the New York theater, that dramatic criticism took a sharp tumble with the dropping out of Woollcott and Broun and the passing of Hammond. Woollcott and Broun, both with many pursuits at hand, quit because they had had enough. Only death took Hammond out of C 1 and 3. In his years as the first reviewer of Illinois and the drama authority of the prairie, he decided that in play reviewing he had a trade and a good one. And he meant to stick to it.

Often producers, playwrights and even actors will speak their minds about play criticism as practiced in New York. Such sayings, when well said, are interesting, and particularly so to the reviewers themselves. Jed Harris, when he gets worked up, will rip into the boys, unmindful of the fact that they were once his darlings.

"There's no man now writing criticism," he told me when I caught him in one of his unsparing moods, "who has any creative force. They're critics only because they have the jobs. When their papers fold up they're no longer critics. There's nothing more false than the idea that a newspaperman is making an advance when he goes from a reportorial job to the rôle of a dramatic critic. The men who've stuck to reporting are the top men of the newspaper world." . . . A gulp of coffee and his blasting continued: "I was always just a fellow trying to master my craft. I have never been disturbed or exhilarated about a review. I never gave a damn what a critic said about me. I've always tried to get young actors and playwrights to promise not to read reviews. The critics by their early raves hurt young Irwin Shaw. Their cracks at Clifford Odets are stupid. If Mr. Odets stopped writing, or if Mr. Sam Harris or Mr. George Kaufman or Mr. McClintic or Mr. Miller stopped producing, they would represent a definite loss to the theater. But if anybody now writing reviews stopped there'd be no notice of it whatsoever. . . . No, wait; I make an honorable exception. There's a critic who once wrote a book about a leisurely world voyage. His name is Atkinson. He is a man of humility and one who realizes that there are things about the theater he doesn't know and doesn't understand."

Channing Pollock is usually quick to blast away at the aisle-sitters, but without really losing his sense of humor. If you talk to him in his West End Avenue apartment he'll pace the floor of his study and let fly:

"I've had thirty Broadway productions if you include my first play, 'The Game of Hearts.' Thirty productions and out of those thirty I've had eight good notices. But I've made a million and a half and I can tell anybody in the world to go to hell. And that includes the critics, who said 'The Fool' was the lousiest play ever written. It earned me half a million and it's on the required reading list of nine universities. The same critics said 'The Enemy' was just as lousy and it sold 26,000 copies in Japan! . . . The other playwrights who've been panned as much as I have are Anne Nichols, Charles Dickens and Ibsen. Well, I say, let 'em pan. I've been in the New York theater for forty years and I've outlived several generations of critics and will outlive several more. Criticism in New York is absurd. The critics are suffering from Broadwayitis. Also, I'd say, from suppressed desires."

Now Robert E. Sherwood takes the stand. His is a more temperate tone. In an interview this ex-critic of *Life* (he did movies and he was good) is the most outspoken of the newer dramatists; he never prefaces a thought with an "This is just between us" or an "But don't print that—." Just prior to the New York opening of "Abe Lincoln in Illinois" I talked with him in Washington. He said:

"The New York critics, if they're erring at all, it's on the side of kindliness. But when you read all the notices, when you take them in a mass, you feel that the critics now suffer from terrific anemia. . . . How I yearn for

Alexander Woollcott and his writings about the theater; for his hat-in-the-air and dancing-in-the-street enthusiasms; for his blind prejudices and his violent nauseas. . . ." He was just getting worked up when the room-service waiter of the Shoreham arrived with the Scotch.

Before going into the roster of the Critics' Circle I'll consider the case of that eminent outsider—A. Woollcott. He was born at Phalanx, N. J., went to a Philadelphia High School and Hamilton College and is now a gentleman of fifty-two years. Of all those writing reviews in New York since the turn of the century—and undoubtedly before—he has done most, to my notion, to stimulate interest in theater-going. He can do more for a book or a play than any man of his time. His printed and spoken enthusiasms have instantaneous and far-reaching cash value. Innumerable instances might be cited: His hurrahs for Katharine Cornell and "A Bill of Divorcement," coming at a time when the play was dying; his discovery of the magazine story called "Goodbye, Mr. Chips"; his street-dancing for Cecilia Loftus, with the result that her mimicry, taken up after years of disuse, became the Sunday-night rage of the town; and, of course, his microphonic hysteria in the case of Ibsen, "A Doll's House" and an actress named Ruth Gordon. "It isn't criticism, it's emotionalism," was the chill comment of a celebrated observer of the drama recently, when the subject of Woollcott's life and works came up. Possibly so, but emotionalism that pays off. There've been times, in dissent, when the Town Crier has protested to no avail. His violent abuse of Eugene O'Neill's "Strange Interlude" did not prevent its becoming that dramatist's greatest success.

Now Woollcott's out of it. Serenely so, he'd have you believe. His immediate concerns are his writing, broadcasting, lecturing and island-owning. He's at work daily around 8 A.M., is happiest when in bed before midnight. He began his play-reviewing, as the *Times's* duly appointed critic, with his coverage of a comedy called "The Rule of Three," of dim and distant memory. He foreswore daily criticism in the late Twenties when he gave up his job on the *World*. He continues his playgoing, if not his first-nighting, whenever he happens to be in the vicinity of playhouses. His fondness for some of the personalities of the theater—the Lunts, Coward, Helen Hayes, Katharine Cornell—will cause him to cross half a continent to see them perform or to spend a few hours in their company. When he's in New York he's generally at the Gotham; when in Vermont, his address is his island in Lake Bomoseen, and when he's wandering about America he's apt to be just anywhere.

But back to the Critics' Circle. And begin with the Circle's president, the man who was writing about plays in New York for one publication and another since 1905, when he was a third-stringer for the *New York Herald*, and started his career with an account of a forgotten something by Lincoln J. Carter called "Bedford's Hope." His name is George Jean Nathan, born in Fort Wayne, Ind., and he's now fifty-seven. He now serves *Newsweek* and *Esquire* and in the intervening years his pieces on the theater have appeared in countless publications, including *The Smart Set*, over which he and H. L. Mencken presided with such gusto for years. Nathan, more than anyone else, has served as a revolutionizing factor in the American theater. He has taken his place as a debunker, dissenter, hokum-hater and passionate foe of the artificial theater. His has been the greatest single influence in changing the trend of the drama, in reshaping and forcing the taste of the playgoers. He has been the protagonist of some of the great talents in the field of playwriting and producing and his championship has contributed mightily to their development. He, more than any other individual, was the mouthpiece of the theater in revolt, a period that began with the presentation of O'Neill's "Beyond the Horizon." He fought for proper appreciation of Shaw and Strindberg and Hauptmann, just as he was later to do for that of Sean O'Casey and Paul Vincent Carroll. He was the leader in the assault against the drama as represented by Augustus Thomas, George Broadhurst and Charles Klein. He has a fine critical mind and represents a weight of background, despite his clownings and his poses, his gestures and his attitudes, all of which are pretty familiar to his colleagues by now. He has never worked for a daily and probably could never have borne up under the grind of daily criticism. He is a man of wide acquaintance both in and out of the theater, but one who, if he has any real warmth, reveals it to but few. He has, definitely, a social side. And, like Watts and Benchley, is quite willing to permit himself the privilege of a good time. He likes good food, good liquor and good company, especially that of pretty young actresses. Two such actresses, plus Nathan and Watts, often make a congenial foursome at Twenty-one, in the sacred corner held for Nathan daily. He has fondness for the company, and high regard for the talents, of Watts, whom he calls, in his whimsical way, "Wattsie." Nathan is a bachelor and always will be. He is a fellow of both plumage and poise. He is seldom fussed, although at times the sly badgerings of fellow critics have come pretty close to achieving it. He is a traveler and always has been. He lives at the Hotel Royalton. His apartment is his workshop.

Upstate New York claims Burns Mantle, oldest of the critics. He will be sixty-six in December, having been born at Watertown, N. Y. in 1873. Mantle is a worker and he loves the theater. He has been with the *Daily News* continuously since 1922. Prior to coming to New York he was in Denver and Chicago, serving both the *Inter-Ocean* and the *Tribune*. He began his Broadway career as critic of the *Evening Mail* and was with that paper until he joined the *News*. Mantle, as a reviewer, is extraordinarily conscientious, somewhat stubborn, and definitely on the kindly side. But there's nothing more devastating than his use of "stars," a device which he put into practice some years ago. One star, two stars or even two and a half stars can generally be taken to mean quick failure for a production. He rarely gives four stars to a play. Burns Mantle is famous, of course, for his annual "Best Plays" and year-book volumes. The series began with the "Best Plays of 1919-20" and has gone on uninterruptedly ever since. The *News'* critic makes his home at Forest Hills. He has a wide acquaintance in the profession and out of it and, what with his books and his writings for the *News*, he puts in a full year's work nearly every year.

John Anderson, born in Pensacola, Fla., is forty-three. As critic of the *Journal and American* he is New York's highest paid reviewer, getting around $17,000, and this is not inclusive, of course, of earnings from outside writings. The only men who ever topped the $17,000 figure, so far as I know, were Woollcott, Percy Hammond and Gilbert Gabriel. With the *Herald Tribune* syndicate returns, Hammond must have soared to $25,000. Anderson came to New York in 1918, did rewrite, reporting and feature stuff for the *Evening Post*, became assistant to the aging

J. Rankin Towse, finally succeeded Towse as critic, and, in 1928, shifted to the *Journal*. He has been there ever since. As a rewrite man—and he has never ceased to be grateful for his city-room training—he was fast and glib. These assets have stuck with him. As a reviewer and as a writer, he has clarity, fluency and force. He is given to wit and to cynicism and has no mercy upon the dreadful little plays which, while they would not have rating among the semi-pros, manage to achieve Broadway production. Anderson, tall, handsome, touchy, super-sensitive, is married to Margaret Breuning, art critic of the *Journal and American*. They have an apartment near the East River and a delightful place in Fairfield County, Conn., some fourteen miles from Bridgeport. Anderson attended the University of Virginia and his family wanted him to be a lawyer. He worked on Pensacola newspapers prior to coming to New York. He writes his reviews at his apartment and the copy is taken to the *Journal and American* by cab, generally the same driver, who calls at 1 A.M. He has had a fling at playwriting—adaptation and translation—and is the author of "The American Theater." He is either writing, or he will write, a novel. He contributes to *Town and Country* and other periodicals. He was last season's winner of *Variety's* Box Score.

Geoffrey Parsons, No. 1 editorial writer of the *Herald Tribune*, who has had a voice and a vote for years in that newspaper's city-room affairs, was in the Little Bar of the Hotel Cleveland during the Republican National Convention of 1936. The matter of the unfilled post of dramatic critic came up. Several other newspapermen were at the table. "Who'll it be, Geoffrey—Dick Watts?" asked Joseph Alsop, Jr. of the Washington staff. Parsons thought a minute and said, well, there'd been the feeling that Watts, although the best qualified of the candidates, was too radical. But, he averred, it would probably be Watts. When the new season began Richard Watts, Jr., born in Charleston, W. Va. and now 41, was in his seat on the aisle as successor to Percy Hammond. Watts, in the opinion of some of his confreres, is a writer with a completely partisan social viewpoint and, although he lives well himself, with every conceivable luxury, he is intolerant of upper class life. He is, however—and I believe his associates will readily concede it—a man who has critical judgment not surpassed in this age. I've known him some fifteen years and now, as in the beginning, I've always believed that he has a feel for the theater that is extraordinary. However he came by it, there's something in his mental composition that's real theater. In his writings he never hesitates to go completely overboard. He can get as excited over a chorus girl as he can over Sean O'Casey. He likes a pretty face but he also likes, and knows, a good play. Watts, of the far-famed blue shirt, has never had actual reportorial experience but in doing his reviews he's as fast as a rewrite man. He writes at the office, waits around for a proof and then hustles down to Bleeck's for a drink. Or even two. Of all the critics, with Benchley excepted, he gets the most fun out of his job. He gets around. He is exciting and provocative as a conversationalist and proficient as a match-game player at Bleeck's, which is his second home. Playwright Jack Kirkland, when he set out to beat up a critic, might have been more successful had he not sailed into Watts in Bleeck's, of all places. Watts isn't married, but talks of it and may yet elope with an ingénue. He lives at 131 Riverside Drive. Bleeck's is his favorite bar, "Broadway" his favorite melodrama, and China the country closest to his heart. He goes there annually and is the most traveled of the present-day critics.

They tell you in Louisville, Ky., where he was born in 1900, that John Mason Brown, in his youth, set himself a goal: he wanted to be a dramatic critic. And so we now find him, doing the plays for the *New York Post*, and one of the country's most active and sought-after lecturers on the theater. His earnings from the lecture platform are probably far in excess of his intake at the *Post*. As a reviewer, he is handicapped by the fact that he has never been a practicing newspaperman. There are times, in the writing of a review, when he takes a column or so to get really going. He's a scholar, enormously intelligent, with a devastating theatrical background. He, too, is merciless at the expense of some of the little nonentities of the drama that seek to pass themselves off as professional theater. In his annoyances, as in anger, he becomes, at times, positively shrill. He is well-liked by his colleagues, is given to distracting use of the pun, and has been described by one of his best friends as a "cotillion leader at heart." He has done several books on the theater. He writes in his apartment, at 14 East Nineteenth Street, where the copy is picked up by messenger.

The *Sun's* critic, Richard Lockridge, was born in St. Joseph, Mo. forty-one years ago. He lives in Washington Place and he also has a house at Brewster, N. Y., where he spends many week-ends. He also writes his reviews at his apartment and they are picked up by *Sun* messenger around 1 A.M. In the between-season periods, Lockridge goes back to his old trade, City Room rewrite, where he's always welcome. As a dramatic critic Lockridge is independent, his perceptions are excellent, and his observations are generally very sound. Several times a year his particular slant on a play will be the most accurate in New York. He is always intelligent in his writing but rarely exciting. Lockridge, like Brown, has gone in for the lecture platform and has done well at it. He wrote a volume on the life of Edwin Booth and he contributes regularly to *The New Yorker*, these pieces including his amusing sketches of that now familiar couple, "Mr. and Mrs. North."

Brooks Atkinson, born in Melrose, Mass., is forty-five. He's slight, wears glasses, generally carries a cane, and has traveled considerably. He was literary editor of the *Times* when he was given the post of dramatic critic and he found himself thrust into a strange new medium. He's now far easier in his job than he was in the beginning and there has been marked improvement in his style and certainly in his showmanship. "Brooks," a fellow critic said of him recently, "is a man who has really learned to write." He's done numerous pieces in recent seasons that have been distinguished for their clarity and beauty. I have in mind, particularly, his review of "The Green Pastures." He's a man of taste, perception and high honesty and a good review from him is of tremendous value at the box office. He's the author of several books including one on Henry Thoreau. "And there are times," said one of his colleagues, "that he really thinks he's a reincarnation of Thoreau." This observation came from an aisle-sitter for whom Atkinson can do no wrong. Atkinson is as conscientious a man as ever held a critic's post. No theater is too far or too obscure for him. He covers everything there is to cover, whether it's in Macdougal Street, in Harlem or in Suffern, on the Hudson's west bank.

Walter Winchell has membership in the Critics' Circle as the official critic of the *Daily Mirror*. Winchell, an American phenomenon, has no theatrical background and has never pretended to have. What with his broadcasting and his column writing and his reputed earnings of $4,000 weekly, reviewing is something of a sideline. Here's a man who, via a daily column printed first in the *Graphic* and later in the *Mirror*, became a craze. He swept the country like the Turkey Trot; he became a national obsession, in the sense of such crazes as the Gibson Girl and the Merry Widow Waltz, and "Yes, We Have No Bananas," which had preceded him, and Mickey Mouse, Snow White and Charlie McCarthy, all of which came along after he had taken hold from coast to coast. So of what importance could mere play reviewing have to such a fellow? He is never certain of himself in his reactions to a play and he is apt to be at extreme odds with his colleagues. One of his minor triumphs was, of course, his stand on "Hellzapoppin'." As an ex-vaudevillian, he loved it and gave it the works. The other critics howled the first night, but their reviews were pieces of only tolerant acceptance. But "Hellzapoppin'," plus Olsen & Johnson, didn't let Winchell down. The show, still running at this writing, was the smash hit of the season.

Robert Benchley is fifty. He was born in Melrose, Mass. and is a fellow of amazing talents. A Harvard man, he was once fired by the *Tribune* when his pay was $40 a week. As a play reviewer, whether for *Life* or *The New Yorker*, he has ranked, for sheer readability, above them all. He has often been handicapped by the fact that he is a comedian and his reviews, whatever else they were, simply had to be amusing. But he is, and always has been, a commentator of soundness in his opinions, whether or not he put them on paper. His services are ever in demand in Hollywood, both as actor and writer. Some day they'll probably discover that he can also run a studio and will put him to doing that.

Sidney B. Whipple, of the *World-Telegram*, is the newcomer of the daily New York reviewers, filling a post that has changed hands several times in recent years. He's small, frail and fifty-one. He went to Dartmouth, did correspondence from London and Paris, edited the *Denver Express* and the *South Bend News-Times*, had charge of the United Press staff covering the Hauptmann trial and spent a year with Charles M. Schwab working on his biography which, says Mr. Whipple, "he was too modest to have printed." The *World-Telegram's* reviewer, not yet sure of himself, gets pushed around by his colleagues, but he has a zest for his job and he works in season and out. He has written several books, including "The Lindbergh Crime."

Brooklyn's first gentleman of the theater is Arthur Pollock, critic of the *Eagle*. He's quiet, shy, extraordinarily conscientious and an able commentator. He's fifty-three and has been with the *Eagle* for twenty-odd years. Born in Brooklyn, he went to high school at Richmond Hill and later to Cornell. He did the English version of Henri Bernstein's play, "Melo," which New York saw at the Ethel Barrymore Theater.

Kelcey Allen, sixty-four, has been with *Women's Wear Daily* for a quarter of a century. He got his start in the theatrical field carrying copy for critics about forty-five years ago, the reviewers of that time including Hilary Bell of the *New York Press*, John R. Stevenson of the old *Daily News* and Dr. Kyle of *The Clipper*. Kelcey Allen was with *The Clipper* for about twenty years and he had charge of the post office that this publication conducted for the profession. He also collected items of drama news. When he started with *Women's Wear* he handled advertising as well as the reviews but the advertising now seems to take care of itself. He lives at 300 West 23rd Street, has an uptown workroom in the Longacre Building which he shares with Bide Dudley and he gets his mail at the Hotel Hermitage, as he has been doing for years. He seldom misses an opening and has probably seen more plays on Broadway than any other member of the Circle. He goes to all the Broadway parties, both screen and stage, and not only bears up under them but has a good time and generally outstays everybody. He takes considerable pride in the fact that he is the only representative of a trade paper belonging to the Circle. He was born in Brooklyn. And, incidentally, Kelcey Allen is not his name. The "Kelcey" was taken from Herbert Kelcey, an actor he always admired. He knows just about everybody in the Broadway area. I've yet to meet the man who didn't like him.

The *New Republic's* man on the aisle is Stark Young, born in Mississippi fifty-eight years ago. He has had an interesting literary career, serving as both instructor and professor of English literature, and having written verse, essays, novels, plays and dramatic criticism. He made a fine translation of Anton Chekhov's "The Sea Gull," which was played by Alfred Lunt and Lynn Fontanne and he achieved definite best-seller rating with the novel, "So Red the Rose." He did play reviews for the *Times* in 1924-25. He is a writer of limitless versatility and as a critic he is completely grounded in the literature and technique of the theater. But he is, I'd say, a critics' critic and not a playgoers' critic. His complexities of style never made him ideal as a commentator for the daily press.

Ruth Woodbury Sedgewick, who served as critic and editor of *Stage*, was born in Oakland, Calif., in 1891. She's lived in New York nearly all her life and has always been a devoted theatergoer. She wrote Katharine Cornell's life story, "I Wanted To Be An Actress." Her home is at 34 Gramercy Park.

The *Theater Arts Monthly* is represented at first nights by its editor—Edith J. R. Isaacs. Mrs. Isaacs, sixty-one, is married to Lewis M. Isaacs, lawyer and musician, and since 1920 she has been editor-in-chief of the magazine. She is also one of its owners. She was born in Milwaukee, served as literary editor of the *Milwaukee Sentinel* and for a time was dramatic critic of *Ainslee's Magazine*. "I've had as much fun out of our magazine," says Mrs. Isaacs, "as the time I've put into it. We've always tried to get out a magazine people would sit down and read—not a subway magazine."

Several men now writing reviews are not members of the Critics Circle. These include Louis Kronenberger of *Time*, Mark Barron of the *Associated Press*, Robert Coleman of the *Daily Mirror* and Jack Pulaski of *Variety*. Coleman substitutes for Winchell when W. W. isn't in town, is too busy with his columns or his broadcasts, or just doesn't want to do a particular show. Barron has, via the *Associated Press*, a nation-wide audience for both his reviews and his Broadway pieces and gets excellent Sunday presentation in some of the country's leading dailies. Barron, aside from his whirl with the Theater Guild, has confined his New York career to newspaper work and was with the *Morning Telegraph* and the *Herald Tribune* before joining the staff of the *A.P.* He was city editor for a time and was sent abroad as war correspondent in Ethiopia. He was decorated by the Italians and, having been stricken with fever in the Somaliland, spent weeks in Italian hospitals. Coleman, born in Bainbridge, Ga., Miriam Hopkins' home town, likes the theater but he seems to have a hard-and-fast rule as to the time of his arrivals at the theater. He doesn't like to reach his seat until 9:05. Eugene Burr covers the plays for *Billboard*. His stuff is interestingly presented; he is both amusing and honest.

Heywood Broun, now a Connecticut farmer, syndicated columnist for the *World-Telegram*, and president of the Newspaper Guild, has tried about everything on a newspaper except setting type. He was a good showman as a reviewer, invariably stimulating, but never interested in permanence in the field. Louis Sherwin, who did the plays for the *Globe* for a time, was thoroughly competent and often Nathanesque in his comments. Kenneth Macgowan, who was also on the *Globe*, went into play production. His career as a producer was taken up in some detail by Joseph Verner Reed in "The Curtain Falls." Macgowan, always intelligent and ever serious, has been a Hollywood producer for some years.

George S. Kaufman did second-string reviews for the *Times* during his years as dramatic editor but he never aspired to the critic's post. John Byram, who has been in Paramount's New York office for some years, was also a *Times* second-stringer—scrupulously fair and generally accurate. Bide Dudley, Quinn Martin, Beauvais Fox, Howard Barnes (the *Herald Tribune's* picture reviewer) and Whitney Bolton, now in Hollywood, put in many evenings in judgment of the Broadway drama.

Charles Darnton, long with the *Evening World*, was

never given to brilliance of prose. He is now doing movie gossip in Hollywood. James Craig covered shows for the *Evening Mail* for a time; he is now an editorial writer with *The Sun*. Stephen Rathbun, Harvard '02, came into newspaper work via the hay and grain business. He joined the *Evening Sun* in 1911, later succeeded Hoffenstein as critic, and was, in turn, succeeded by Woollcott. Rathbun has given up newspaper work. Robert Gilbert Welch, who liked nearly every play, was drowned in Bermuda. Unable to swim himself, he went to the rescue of another bather. Robert Garland, who came to New York from Baltimore did the shows for the *World-Telegram* for several years. He had a certain vitality, some definite ideas and a quality that made him generally readable. Douglas Gilbert of the *World-Telegram* staff did a spell of reviewing prior to the coming of Sidney Whipple. John Corbin, who served the *Times* in the post-Woollcott period, was professorial and fussy, and with little theatrical feeling. Charles Brackett did play pieces for *The New Yorker*, and turned in an amusing job of it, but he wasn't a critic of Benchley's depth. Before the steadying Burns Mantle came along the *Daily News* tried James Whittaker, who was married to Ina Claire. There were many of the gossip-wise about Broadway who got their first news of the marriage in a review Whittaker wrote of an Ina Claire play. It was a review that didn't make the home life of the Whittakers any easier.

St. John Ervine came over from London as guest critic on the *World* in the late Twenties. He tried the second-day revue stunt and got away with it rather well. He was, and is, one of the ablest of the commentators, but he had difficulty, particularly in the beginning, in expressing himself for American playgoers. One of his greatest Broadway enthusiasms, oddly enough, was Philip Dunning's shoddy melodrama, "Night Hostess."

Walter Prichard Eaton, Clayton Hamilton, Robert Littel, Channing Pollock, and Frederic McKay are others who have now drifted from the Broadway field. Eaton, a professor turned reviewer, was a thorough critic, and with something of a moral inheritance from William Winter. Clayton Hamilton, a man of broad theatrical background, has served the stage in nearly every capacity except as an actor. Channing Pollock, in his writings for the *Green Book*, long since gone its way, was fluent and stimulating. He liked his job and he made you feel that he did. McKay turned to theatrical management. He has been living at Provincetown the past two years. Littel vanished from criticism with the passing of the *World*.

Jack Lait, who wrote with vitality, and who was a playwright in spare moments, did many reviews for *Variety*. So did Sime and Abel Green, who has been in editorial charge of that vigorous weekly for some years. And there was, and is, Matthew White, Jr. He covered shows for *Munsey's Magazine*. When I last heard from him he was living in Westport. In a letter he recalled that he saw his first play in Salt Lake City in the middle Sixties—one in which Annie Adams Kiskadden played—and that Brigham Young saw it too, sitting halfway down the aisle in a rocking chair.

Many of those who have given critical service, distinguished and otherwise, to the New York theater in this century have passed on. . . . William Winter, Alan Dale, Louis V. DeFoe, C. M. S. McLellan, Acton Davies, James Garrison, J. Rankin Towse, Hamilton Ormsby, James L. Metcalfe, Arthur Hornblow, Arthur Ruhl, Adolph Klauber, E. W. Osborn, Leo Marsh, Lawrence Reamer, Leander Richardson, Harriet Quimby, Sime Silverman, Norman Hapgood, Franklin Fyles.

Alan Dale, according to present-day ratings, could make or break a show. People read him. He was flamboyant, brazen, affected, smart-alecky. He once wrote a play on his own account, "Madonna of the Future." It had definite quality but it failed quickly. William Winter, a voluminous critic, and a man of intellect and understanding, wrote endlessly of Shakespearian plays and players. J. Rankin Towse, who started as a boy actor in England, was writing reviews for the *Evening Post* when he was past eighty. The impression that we have today of Louis V. DeFoe is that he was definitely on the dull side. Rennold Wolf was critic, wit, playwright, first-nighter, man-about-town and columnist. Acton Davies had a following as the reviewer for the *Evening Sun*. Franklin Fyles, who was with the *Morning Sun*, died in 1911. He went in for playwriting and with David Belasco wrote, "The Girl I Left Behind Me," which opened the Empire Theater. Arthur Ruhl did pieces for *Collier's* and later for the *Herald Tribune*. Arthur Hornblow, father of Arthur Hornblow, Jr., now a producer-executive at Paramount, wrote for the *Theater Magazine*, of which he was editor.

Lawrence Reamer, native of Louisville, Ky., died in 1928 after more than twenty years service as critic of drama and music. He served the *Sun*, the *Herald* and the *Evening Sun*, and was far more interested in music than in the theater.

And who are the critics of the big out-of-New-York dailies? Let's make a quick tour of what the showmen call the "key cities."

CHICAGO: Lloyd Lewis, judged by New York standards, is the ablest of the Chicago commentators. He's with the *Daily News*. He is a Civil War historian on the side. Ashton Stevens, the Senior Loop critic, serves the *Herald American*; Cecil Smith the *Tribune*, Claudia Cassidy the *Journal of Commerce* and Robert Pollak the *Daily Times*. Ashton Stevens was with the *Herald Examiner* for years and has a wide following. The summer of 1939 saw the passing of Amy Leslie, eighty-four, who retired in 1930 as dramatic critic of the *Daily News* after forty years of service. Edwin Booth, Bernhardt, Lillian Russell, John Drew and Richard Mansfield were among her friends.

BOSTON: Charles Howard, eighty-four, has been reviewing plays for the *Globe* for half a century. Edward Harkins, of the *Boston Daily Record* has been at it for approximately thirty years. The critic's chair on the *Evening Transcript*, which the late H. T. Parker filled with such distinction, is now occupied by John K. Hutchens, formerly of the *New York Times*. The other first-nighters of the Common are Elliot Norton of the *Boston Post*, Elinor Hughes of the *Herald*, Peggy Doyle of the *American* (who succeeded George Holland, columnist, when he was barred from the Boston theaters by the Shuberts), Helen Eager of the *Traveler* and Leslie A. Sloper of the *Christian Science Monitor*.

PHILADELPHIA: Linton Martin of the *Inquirer* is Philadelphia's best known critic. He formerly covered music. Robert Sensenderfer, who saw long service as sports editor of the *Evening Bulletin* does the plays for that paper. Jeff Keen who also does general feature work, reviews for the *Daily News*; Ed Schloss, who handles music as well as drama, represents the *Record* and Harry Murdock does plays and films for the *Evening Ledger*.

CLEVELAND: William F. McDermott, critic of the *Plain Dealer*, has high rating. Some years ago, when that daily was seeking "the best man in America who is not in New York," some of the country's leading showmen were asked to assist in the selection of the new critic. All votes, seemingly, went to McDermott, who had been working in Detroit. McDermott now writes on many subjects and takes frequent trips abroad, sending his pieces from London, Paris, Cairo, Indo-China and points east.

CINCINNATI: E. B. Radcliffe, born in Worcester, Mass., does the plays for Cincinnati's leading daily, the *Enquirer*. He has been a member of the local staff for two years or so. He succeeded Herman Berns, who gave up art and went into trade. Berns is now associated with New York's *Twenty-one Club*, of which his brother, Charlie Berns, is one of the partners.

ATLANTA: Three dailies continue in the Atlanta field. Frank Daniel is critic of the *Journal*, Lee Rogers of the *Constitution* and Dudley Glass of the *Georgian*. Glass has been covering the drama off and on for twenty-five years. Atlanta still gets nearly all the plays that come south of the Potomac. The shows go into the Erlanger Theater, only a block or so away from the Hotel Georgian-Terrace, still proudly standing at Peachtree and Ponce de Leon Avenue.

OTHER OUTPOSTS: Nelson B. Bell, critic of the *Washington Post* also does films, and is one of the most industrious of the out-of-town commentators. Gilbert E.

Kanour of the *Baltimore Evening Sun* and Norman Clark of the *News-Post* cover whatever Broadway sends to Baltimore's two playhouses. Len G. Shaw is well known as critic of the *Detroit Free-Press* and so is Boyd Martin of Louisville's *Courier-Journal*. Martin also covers motion pictures, takes trips to Hollywood, directs social and collegiate productions, and entertains constantly at his home for visiting notables. Pittsburgh has a live man in Harold Cohen of the *Post-Gazette*. St. Louis' leading reviewer is Colvin McPherson of the *Post-Dispatch*. Memphis' playgoers look to Harry Martin, serving the *Commercial Appeal*, for their drama comment and Dallas and the Southwest seem to swear by John Rosenfield of the *Dallas Morning News*. Richmond, Va., has a capable commentator in Edith Lindeman. Samuel T. Wilson is No. 1 man in Columbus, O., writing for the *Dispatch*. The town of Des Moines, which once gave Helen Hayes the staggering gross of $9,400 for a single performance of "Victoria Regina," reads Kenneth Clayton, who is with the *Register-Tribune*. There's a man at New Haven, Harold M. Bone, *Variety's* representative, who has a sharp eye for box-office values.

The Pacific Coast's reviewers include Edwin Schallert of the *Los Angeles Times* and John Hobart of the *San Francisco Chronicle*. Canada's aisle-seat authorities are S. Morgan Powell of the *Montreal Star* and Augustus Bridle of the *Toronto Star*.

So there we are. Those are the dramatic critics of our land and our time. I've made no attempt to include mention of all the commentators, able and otherwise, who have reviewed for the across-America newspapers. But I don't believe I've missed many serving the New York field since 1900.

So, in considering the personnel of the Critics' Circle, as of 1939, you reach these conclusions:

New York critics like their jobs. They hold them indefinitely. They live a long time. Their ages now range from the middle thirties to the middle sixties. Their pay ranges from less than $5,000 a year to around $17,000. Their opportunities for income via outside writing are many, and most of them are engaged in extra-curricular endeavor. And, I repeat, the membership in the Circle, taken as a whole, is one of high competence. And the job of dramatic critic is one of the pleasantest forms of livelihood that this republic affords. Pleasant, profitable and one that should appeal to people of talent, taste and intelligence. It's all of that, but try and get it!

The critics have their place in the Broadway picture; but so have the columnists, the press agents, the casting agents, the Glamour Girls (debs, sub-debs and otherwise) and the inn-keepers.

Consider the columnists: The *Herald Tribune*, realizing that something should be done about the coverage of the frivolous side of New York life, let Lucius Beebe go ahead with his once-a-week feature, "This New York." His column is eagerly read by a limited New York clientele and it is prominently displayed in the few out-of-town papers in which it appears. It's one that would probably have been considered daring by an earlier generation and I often feel that Beebe's mood is one of impatience with the present-day scene and that his real interest lies in the grandeur of a bygone day. Leonard Lyons, who does the "Lyons Den" for the *New York Post*, is a persistent little man, inept as a writer, but a conscientious news-digger. Louis Sobol, of the *Journal and American*, was once of and for Broadway, entirely. But, with the acquisition of a flock of the O. O. McIntyre papers, his style changed overnight. An able, affable and kindly fellow, Sobol. If he's less readable for his metropolitan public than he was when he was concerned solely with night-life recordings, it's a penalty that he must have expected. Danton Walker, of the *Daily News*, and once Alexander Woollcott's secretary, is one of the more recent recruits to the columning field. He looks well in a white tie and does a nice job of following the Winchell pattern. George Ross does theater news and night life for the *World-Telegram*. He was once a supper-club press agent and is without reportorial experience. His column is often a mosiac of drama news notes and items on the state of the cosmos. If he appears to take himself pretty seriously, it's perhaps forgivable in view of the latter-day glorification of columnists. I've never met or even danced the rumba with Dorothy Kilgallen. She follows the prescribed Broadway routine, often brightly and energetically.

Press agents: Richard Maney, as I've intimated, leads the pack. When he isn't handling five or six shows simultaneously he calls it a dull season. There are numerous others given to dexterity in the press-agent field—William Fields, Bernard Sobel (once Ziegfeld's Glorifier and now with Metro), Charles Washburn, Irving Hoffman, Steve Hannagan (old Mr. Sun Valley himself), Ted Saucier, Arthur J. Levy, Karl Bernstein, Joseph Ryle, Phyllis Perlman and the wistful Mike Goldreyer, who's been doing "Tobacco Road" for so long I'm sure he could play Jeeter Lester himself.

Casting agents: Few of them are worth their salt. Those best-known include Briscoe & Goldsmith, Richard Pitman, Sam Lyons, Louis Schurr, Dorothy Vernon (a song and dance girl herself before she switched careers), Jane Broder, the William Morris office and the Leland Hayward office.

Glamour girls: The town's debs and sub-debs get about. They get their publicity, expect it, and like it. Their favorite Americans, besides Sherman Billingsley and the brothers Kriendler, are the columnists. There'll be a battle for Brenda Frazier honors during the winter. Who'll be debutante No. 1? Well, pick one out of these ten: Elise Cavanagh, Patricia Plunkett, Nancy Saunders, Dolly von Stade, Joan Townsend, Helene D. Coler, Cynthia S. Myrick, Lois Warner, Katherine Hamill, Joan K. Martin.

Most of them, perhaps all of them, will descend these winter evenings upon the Stork Club. There they'll undoubtedly find that the strongest competition will be afforded in the person of a young woman whose father was captain of the Brooklyn Fire Department. She's animated and slim and five feet two. Her thick dark hair is worn in a loose bob, shoulder length. She's not a debutante and certainly she never wanted to be. But she's something of New York's year-round Glamour Girl. Her name is Eleanor Holm. By the time these lines appear it may have been changed to Mrs. Billy Rose.

## Summing-Up

NOVEMBER OF 1939, LATE NOVEMBER, COMPLETES MY
twentieth year in New York. I came North rather young,
somewhat terrified, and with a feeling of great excitement
and tremulousness for the city itself. Such feeling has
diminished only partially with the passing years. These
years have been incredibly swift. It seems only a few afternoons ago that I got off a train in the maze of the Pennsylvania Station and soon was gazing upon Seventh Avenue, a sea of snow and slush.

I've lived in three of the five boroughs, and in numerous
parts of Manhattan Island: Morningside Heights, Washington Heights, the East Fifties, the East Sixties, Murray
Hill, Times Square and even at the Statue of Liberty,
commuting daily via those little white boats. In leaving the
city on my many long jaunts I've often had the feeling
that it was just too overpowering, and that I couldn't stand
it indefinitely, but I've always rushed back to it. I like
revisiting Georgia, state of my birth, at every opportunity,
but New York's my town. It's home.

I like the din of it. I like its sleekness and its tawdriness,

its grace and its gaucheries. I enjoy listening to little
snatches of talk on the subways, elevators and escalators,
and watching the people, those of glossy exterior and those
who also have that Fourteenth Street look. I like to hear
the sea sounds at the Battery and the soft purr of 2 A.M.
traffic along Park Avenue. I like to wander about Fort
Tryon Park and gaze out upon the sweep of the Hudson;
to stroll through Sutton Place and along the margins of
the island; to get the full feel of the city's beauty, which
is rare and incommunicable, in the vicinity of the Plaza,
and to take late afternoon rides on Second Avenue's surviving "L" when the traffic is going the other way. I've always
been fascinated by Yorkville and its Czech and German
restaurants, by the Spuyten Duyvil hilltop and by the
vista of Manhattan from the rim of the Palisades.

You can never see all of New York. Not that you'd
want to, but its very elusiveness is one of its challenges.
It's been years since I've explored Greenwich Village. I've
done Harlem only twice since my quest of Marcus Garvey
nearly twenty years ago. One trip to the Metropolitan
Museum and one to the Museum of Natural History are
my credits on the side of culture and learning. I get to
Chinatown several times a year and to Coney Island once
or twice. My job is Times Square, the world's greatest
midway. I've occasionally tried the bowling alleys and the
shooting galleries but the dime-a-dance halls and the auc-
tion sales are for evenings still ahead of me.

For thirteen years, as of November of '39, I've been writing the "Broadway After Dark" column for *The Sun*. I still have my same desk in the southwest corner of the City Room and my same telephone extension, 362. In these thirteen years Broadway's changes—changes of trend, method and personnel—have come gradually, but, taken as a whole, and in retrospect, they're startling.

Playhouses have vanished. Play production has dwindled to half of what it was. Great newspapers have disappeared. Famous figures of the Broadway field have passed on. Winthrop Ames, Dillingham, Erlanger, Ziegfeld, Belasco, Sime Silverman, Blinn, Jeanne Eagels—they all have gone. But a new surge of talent and a new array of producing units have come along. The Group Theater and the Playwrights' Company as organizations; Lillian Hellman, Robert E. Sherwood, Maxwell Anderson, Clifford Odets, Moss Hart, William Saroyan, Albert Johnson, Margaret Webster, Katharine Hepburn and many others as individuals.

Gossip columnists have taken the town. The autograph chasers have laid the Forties low. Broadway has rediscovered Shakespeare and Ibsen. Hollywood has discovered Shaw. The Lunts, Katharine Cornell and Helen Hayes have developed with the years. George M. Cohan holds his place as the First Citizen of Theatertown. Smash hits run longer than they ever did. Inferior plays vanish within a week. The 8:30 curtain has been supplanted by the curtain at 8:45. The $5.50 box-office top has given way to the $4.40 (in rare cases), the $3.30 and the $2.20. And even as low as $1.65 on the road.

The midtown map has been severely altered. The Hippodrome, haggard and untenanted, was recently demolished. The Criterion is gone and you'd look in vain for the Casino, the Knickerbocker, the Thirty-ninth Street and the Century. Forty-second Street now hides its face beneath the shambles of burlesque; the legitimate stage has fled the thoroughfare. Forty-fifth Street has become Broadway's first tributary. The Palace, once the pride of vaudeville, is a second-run movie house. Several institutions, however—such as the Algonquin, Sardi's, Dinty Moore's, the Lambs Club—have defied change. They have remained just as they were.

I shall try to look back over thirteen years of Broadway coverage and present the findings as they occur to me. The most soul-satisfying evenings I've had in the theater came with the seeing of such plays as "What Price Glory," "Broadway," "Rain" and "The Green Pastures." But if I could recall to the stage just one player to give one performance for a final night of drama before Manhattan Island slid into the sea, I would shout for the return of William Gillette in the rôle of Sherlock Holmes. I share, whole-heartedly, the critics' recognition of Cornell, Hayes and the Lunts as the foremost players of the present-day theater and feel, most assuredly, that exciting drama will be forthcoming from the newer playwrights.

Stars of tomorrow, surely, will emerge from the ranks of the outstanding young talent of the moment: Katharine Hepburn, Mildred Natwick, Dean Jagger, Jose Ferrer, Burgess Meredith, Louise Platt, Kent Smith, Uta Hagen, Jessica Tandy, Adele Longmire, Marcy Westcott, Helen Trenholme, Katherine Emery, Anne Revere, Julie Haydon, Eleanor Lynn, Lenore Lonergan, Van Heflin, Joseph Cotten, Helen Claire, Gene Tierney, Art Smith, and young Bronson Dudley, another member of the Bide Dudley tribe.

I no longer crave first nights. I've attended my twelve hundred or so and am now content with a dozen a season. The good ones. For the past two seasons I've been going pretty steadily to third and fourth nights. I like seeing certain scenes of plays over and over again; I never tired of portions of "Idiot's Delight," "Of Mice and Men" and of "Oscar Wilde," which is something to be remembered because of the lucency of Robert Morley's performance. I've seldom beheld a footlights personality as attractive as Katharine Hepburn as she appeared in "The Philadelphia Story." I consider Morris Carnovsky of the Group Theater a fine actor and James T. Powers has always been one of the funniest men who ever set foot upon a stage. I yearn for the return of Joe Cook in a show as good as his tricks and I hope to see Miriam Hopkins back on Broadway, not in a play merely to be playing it, but in something befitting her abundant talents. I don't know of another young actress, or an old one, who has her quality of sudden iridescence, which casts its spell not only over the audience but over all the other players.

I have consuming admiration for such people of the present-day theater as Guthrie McClintic, George S. Kaufman, Dwight Deere Wiman, Arthur Hopkins, Vinton Freedley, Brock Pemberton, Lewis E. Gensler, Stanley Gilkey, Harry Kline, Johnson Briscoe, Gene Buck, Richard Aldrich, Billy Gaxton, Sam H. Harris and, of course, William A. Brady. I've yet to meet a showman who was not ardent in his praise of Sam Harris. I think the prankful brothers Krimsky have proved their stuff at the American Music Hall and should now invade Broadway. I'm forever interested in the showmanship of Billy Rose, whether he's staging an Aquacade, a Frontier Centennial or marrying Eleanor Holm. I get from Katharine Cornell, to a far greater extent than from any other performer, a sense of the theater's glamour, now and everlasting.

There are also words, for these final pages, about newspapers and newspapermen. I have high regard for many who have come within my experience. Certainly for W. G. Sutlive and J. P. Miller of Savannah, John Paschall and Angus Perkerson of Atlanta, James Wright Brown of

New York, Paul Bellamy and John S. McCarrens of Cleveland, John S. Knight of Akron, and Keats Speed, Edmond Bartnett, Edwin C. Hill, Owen Oliver, Peter A. Dolan, and Bob Peck, all of New York.

Newspapermen read newspapers, and wherever they happen to be. I see nearly all of the New York papers every day. I like the clarity of Anne O'Hare McCormick's pieces in the *Times*. I'm a follower of Daniel and Joe Williams in the *World-Telegram*. I think Frank Graham of *The Sun* gets out a grand sports column and I seldom miss the copy and the comment of *The Sun*'s H. I. Phillips, who has a large cross-America following. I've found Edmund DeLong of this same newspaper to be an able reporter. Ditto Mabel Greene. I think Meyer Berger of *The Times* is a news writer of high attainments and have admiration for the talents of Morris Markey, once of the *Atlanta Journal* and *The New Yorker*. Stanley Walker, now of the Philadelphia *Public Ledger* and Mark Ethridge of the *Louisville Courier-Journal* are the only reporters I've ever known who can sell themselves as executives and as editors, and then demonstrate capacities for their new posts. I'm perhaps not as expert as I should be in fashions, but it's my notion that Kay Thomas of *The Sun* and Katherine Vincent of the *Herald Tribune*, are better-looking, and undoubtedly better-dressed, than most of the women of whom they write.

Now where? And what?

I shall probably always stay in newspaper work, regardless of other activities. The feel for it, the zest for it, is not something that you acquire; it's something that's always been a part of you. I find that I have retained all of the excitement and enterprise and wide-eyed curiosity that I had when I was doing police reporting in Atlanta. Since the day I first went to work in that dingy second-floor City Room of the *Press*, Whitaker Street, Savannah, I have never for an instant had the slightest desire to leave the newspaper field, not even when there was a swimming pool at my California doorstep and the movies were paying me $200 a day.

I now want to do many things. I want to drive again across America; to call at the Elks lodge in Roanoke and see if my old friend the undertaker is still around; to revisit George Ade Davis on his great ranch in the oil country of Oklahoma, and to return to Idaho's wilds, amid the peaks of the Yellow Jackets, for that deer I never got. I'd like another crack at Hollywood. I want to go to Tibet and Afghanistan and to Sorrento; I'd like to drive from Cape Town to Cairo, to go back to the Dead Sea and look up little Mr. Saad and wander through Germany, from end to end, writing all I see and hear and feel.

Also, I'd like to take a leisurely and long-deferred trip down the Mississippi by barge, and I'll probably do it. I'd

like to have a little place, just a shack, in the fastnesses of
Maine, or along the coastline, and I'll probably get it.

The clocks have spun back. That Peachtree station,
Atlanta, seems only the day before yesterday. . . . Gains-
ville, Salisbury, Danville, Lynchburg, Washington, Baltimore and the Pennsylvania Station—New York! . . .
Here it is, late summer of 1939. Here am I, stripped to
the waist, hiding out and pounding away—always that last-
minute rush to meet and to make a deadline.

But I was about to forget something. Besides those plans
for wandering all over the map, I also want to write another play. It will be a very special kind of play this time.
It may not need any scenery and there may not be any
actors. And I won't care whether it has a first act or a
third. But, God willing, it's going to have a second! . . .
Now let's see. It's to be called "U. S. 40." The locale is
Utah. The time is forty-five minutes past eight. And when
the curtain rises ——

And this, perhaps, is the very minute for me to be getting at it.